IT PROJECT MANAGEMENT ESSENTIALS

IT PROJECT MANAGEMENT ESSENTIALS: INTRODUCTION TO IT PROJECT MANAGEMENT

IT products and services play an essential part in most businesses. Companies require reliable Internet and network connections to communicate with their employees and customers. They use software applications to monitor their projects, and computerized equipment to build their products and supply their services.

An IT project is essentially a project that delivers a new or improved IT product or service. Like all projects, it has a definite beginning and end, and it results in a noticeable change. To succeed, the IT project has to be managed through all its phases.

Because companies rely on IT so much, it's vital that IT projects succeed. A failure, such as the breakdown of an internal IT system, or the release of a faulty software application, is often a highly visible failure. This can negatively affect a company's reputation in the market and lead to lost sales and customer dissatisfaction. A successful IT infrastructure is essential to business success. And IT project management helps ensure the success of all IT processes and products.

Traditional project management processes and techniques can be applied to any IT environment. However, the project manager must have a good grasp of the unique challenges of IT projects.

To succeed, IT projects have to be carefully managed through all phases, from Initiation to Closure.

In this course, you'll learn about how IT project managers can use project management tools, such as the work breakdown structure and Gantt charts, to plan and monitor their IT projects. These tools enable project managers to deliver an effective IT infrastructure to their organization.

Introduction to IT Project Management
1. The Value of IT Project Management
2. IT Project Phases
3. Project Management Tools

THE VALUE OF IT PROJECT MANAGEMENT

1. Introducing projects

When people think of projects, they usually think of work projects. But have you ever considered how many projects take place around you? Consider these examples. Your neighbor builds a new house. Your sister organizes a family vacation overseas. Your son's class puts on a school play. Your community holds a charity fair. Your local government upgrades the roads in your area. These are all examples of projects.

It's likely you were able to come up with a list of several projects. Companies usually have a number of projects taking place at the same time. Some of these might be clearly visible, such as building a new factory or expanding an office.

Other projects are linked to immediate business commitments. For instance, a company might have to make 1,000 products by the end of the month in order to meet customer demand. Or it might need to undertake a review of its accounts in preparation for an audit.

And some projects are linked to ongoing, rather than immediate, goals. These projects include recruiting and training staff and updating company guidelines in order to improve quality of service.

What exactly is a project? Actually, there are many definitions, and trying to understand them all can get confusing. At its simplest, a project is a temporary undertaking that results in a visible change. In other words, a project has a definite beginning and end. The aim of a project is to create something new or different.

Question

A CEO is outlining some of the work her company is undertaking. Which of her statements refer to projects?

Options:

1. "We're committed to delivering quality to our customers."
2. "We'll retain our current staff levels for the next year."
3. "We're upgrading our billing system over the next six months."
4. "At the end of this month, we'll have produced 500 processors."

Answer

Option 1: This option is incorrect. A project must have a definite time frame.

Option 2: This option is incorrect. A project must result in a tangible change.

Option 3: This option is correct. This is a project that will result in a changed billing system within a set time.

Option 4: This option is correct. This project will result in new products within a clear time frame.

All projects have a number of characteristics:

- they're unique undertakings
- they're made up of interdependent activities
- they create a quality deliverable, and
- they involve multiple resources that require close co-ordination

Consider the company that produces processors. This month, it has a unique project to deliver 500 customized processors. As with all projects, it has to deliver the processors to a high standard of quality.

To complete the project, the team carries out numerous interdependent activities, including sourcing raw materials and supplies and building and testing the processors. This involves a coordinated effort between many resources in the company.

Many companies carry out IT projects. IT projects involve obvious components such as technology, including software applications and computer hardware. However, they also involve many other components, such as training, communication, testing, and deployment. One of the goals of an IT project is to ensure that all these components are integrated into a total, functional, and usable system.

Question

What are the characteristics of a project?

Options:

1. A unique undertaking
2. Made up of interdependent activities
3. Creates a quality deliverable
4. Involves multiple resources
5. Continues indefinitely
6. Must lead to increased profits

Answer

Option 1: This option is correct. A project is a unique undertaking with a definite objective.

Option 2: This option is correct. Completing a project involves carrying out numerous interdependent activities, such as research, production, testing, and delivery.

Option 3: This option is correct. A project must deliver a tangible result, such as a new product or an improved service.

Option 4: This option is correct. A project team is needed to complete a project.

Option 5: This option is incorrect. A project must have a definite beginning and end.

Option 6: This option is incorrect. A project might lead to increased profits. However, projects may also be undertaken to improve processes, retrain staff, and expand the business or enhance its reputation.

2. IT and non-IT projects

Organizations usually have a number of projects underway at

the same time. These projects can often be divided into two categories – IT projects and non-IT projects. For example, a company might have a project to restructure its teams and a project to upgrade the software that its finance department uses. IT projects and non-IT projects have different characteristics. Understanding these differences enables you to improve the way you manage any project.

Non-IT projects usually have a dedicated team and a well-defined priority. They are months or even years long. And the technological risk is often constant during the course of the project.

Dedicated team

Depending on the organization structure, non-IT projects usually have a dedicated team. In other words, the people on that team work only on that team and they're not shared with other projects. Once the project is complete, the team members then move on to other projects.

Well-defined priority

Because a non-IT project usually has a dedicated team, it's easier to set priorities. The team's attention isn't split by having to manage different priorities for different projects. Everyone on the team knows the priorities and they're committed to them.

Months or years long

Non-IT projects tend to be longer than IT projects. They have teams that develop over time. Some projects, such as continuous improvement projects, might go on for years. However, this doesn't mean that these projects continue indefinitely. All projects must have a definite end date.

Constant technological risk

In non-IT projects, the technological risks tend to be constant. This doesn't necessarily mean that these projects involve less risk than IT projects. Rather, it means that the risk is invariable and predictable.

This is because non-IT projects usually involve minimal technological changes. The same technology – for example, a stable collaboration database platform to store and exchange files – is used throughout the duration of the project.

T projects have a number of characteristics that make them different from non-IT projects:

- the project team is shared with other projects and with daily operations
- they're usually weeks, and occasionally months, long, but rarely years long
- the team members have multiple priorities that often change, and
- the technological risk is different across different projects

Shared project team

In an IT project, the project team members are often on loan. They're brought into the project because of their specialist IT knowledge. But they're also expected to continue their day-to-day duties.

For example, they might carry out their usual support roles during the morning, and work on the project team in the afternoon.

Weeks or months long

IT projects are usually shorter than non-IT projects. This is because they don't have a dedicated team. IT managers want to get their projects completed quickly, while the resources are available.

Multiple priorities

Team members on IT projects are often balancing multiple priorities at the same time. They might work on more than one project team. Or they might be trying to work around their project priorities and their core daily priorities. Often, their priorities change from day to day, depending on which project manager they're talking to.

Different technological risk

The technological risks in an IT project tend to change as the project progresses. This is because technology is always changing, sometimes very quickly.

Most IT projects involve improving existing technology or developing brand new technology. An IT project to develop new technology is likely to face constantly changing levels of technological risk as new glitches are discovered and addressed.

Consider a company that's looking to develop new graphic design software products. An IT project team is set up and given six months to come up with a new product. However, many of the team members have to spend a lot of time supporting existing versions of the software. Some find it difficult to cope with the conflicting schedules between their project work and their regular work. As the project develops, they find more software bugs that have to be investigated.

Now consider a non-IT project in the same company. Management decides to set up a project team to translate their existing product offerings on their e-commerce sites in both French and Spanish.

The company sets up a dedicated team to research and start translating products in different phases over the next two years. The team is given a set of clear priorities at the start of the project.

The team selects a number of software programs to track its progress for the duration of the project. All team members are trained on how to use these programs.

The IT project was shorter than the non-IT project, and it didn't have a dedicated team.

Unlike the non-IT project, the IT project had to cope with conflicting priorities from other projects.

There's very little technological risk on the non-IT project because all team members are using the same software for the duration of the project. On the IT project, the technological risks are changing all the time as new bugs are discovered.

Question

IT and non-IT projects have different characteristics. Match each characteristic to the type of project it describes. Each project may have more than one match.

Options:

    A.   The project has a dedicated team and the project lasts for months or even years

    B.   The project has a shared team and the project lasts for weeks or months

    C.   The project has a well-defined priority and the technological risk is often constant for the project duration

    D.   The project has multiple priorities and the technological risk changes as the project progresses

Targets:

    1. Non-IT project

    2. IT project

Answer

Non-IT projects have dedicated team members who usually stay with the project until it ends. The team usually works toward one clearly defined priority. Non-IT projects can go on for months or even years, because they have a dedicated team. These projects tend to use the same technology for the duration of the project, so the technological risk is constant.

IT projects often have team members on loan from other teams. Because of this, team members often have conflicts between the team priorities and their other priorities. Because they don't have dedicated teams, IT projects usually don't last longer than a few months. Because of the array of changing technologies involved in the projects, the technological risk is variable.

3. Benefits of IT project management

Project management differs from traditional management in a number of ways. Traditionally, managers are expected to carry out four key functions. They are involved in planning business processes and making key decisions. The next step involves organizing people and resources. The other management functions are leading and controlling. All four functions are carried

SORIN DUMITRASCU

out on an ongoing basis.

Project management involves the four key functions of planning, organizing, leading, and controlling. However, it carries them out in a set time frame.

The project management effort begins with initiating the project. This gives the project a set start date.

And it ends with terminating the project. Remember, projects can't continue indefinitely. They must have a definite end.

Successful project management is a blend of skills, abilities, and knowledge.

For a project to succeed, it must deliver the agreed upon product or service on schedule and within budget using the available resources.

Project managers are expected to plan, monitor, and control projects so that their results meet customer or stakeholder expectations.

A project manager usually carries out a number of activities:

- identifies the requirements of the project which are needed to meet the customer's needs
- establishes project objectives that are clear and achievable
- controls project progress, including quality, cost, scope, and time, and
- addresses stakeholder concerns by changing the project as necessary

But a project is more than just data on a spreadsheet. Successful project management requires successful people management.

One of the key functions of a project manager is to manage team members and ensure that they can achieve the project's objectives. If conflict develops between the team members, the project manager must be able to deal with it.

The project manager also has to deal with other people, including customers, stakeholders, and other managers. Managing the diverse needs of all these people can be a major challenge for any project manager.

Question

Which activities are usually carried out by a project manager?

Options:

1. Setting objectives for the project team
2. Controlling the budget
3. Negotiating with stakeholders
4. Setting customer requirements
5. Marketing the project deliverable

Answer

Option 1: *This option is correct. The project manager sets the objectives for the project team. These objectives must be clear and achievable.*

Option 2: *This option is correct. The project manager must control various aspects of the project, including budget, risk, and quality.*

Option 3: *This option is correct. The project manager must negotiate with the many project stakeholders, including customers, investors, and management.*

Option 4: *This option is incorrect. The project manager identifies the project requirements that must be in place to ensure that the project meets customer requirements. However, the project manager doesn't set the customer requirements. The customer does that.*

Option 5: *This option is incorrect. The project manager must ensure the project deliverable is achieved. What happens after that is outside the scope of the project.*

Now that you have a good grasp of project management, consider what IT project management involves.

IT project management is a form of project management where information technology plays a large part in determining the project's success.

Remember, information technology includes both software and hardware, as well as the various processes and functions that support them.

To manage an IT project successfully in your organization, you need to apply basic project management principles.

However, you also have to modify these principles to meet the needs of your organization. Your organization might have certain processes for managing and evaluating team members.

To apply these skills in an IT project means you have to take into account the characteristics of an IT project, such as the fact that you might not have a dedicated team.

Managing IT projects isn't always easy. Every day, you're likely to face new challenges. For instance, you may have to deal with conflicting priorities among team members. Also, there's often a lack of team development in IT projects.

Conflicting priorities

Team members on IT projects often have other commitments. They have to find a balance between team deadlines and their core functions, such as providing customer support or maintaining internal IT systems.

This can lead to conflicting priorities. The project manager is committed to meeting the project deadline, but team members might have other more pressing commitments on other projects.

Lack of team development

IT projects are usually shorter than non-IT projects. Because of this, the project manager often doesn't have the time to engage in traditional team development activities with team members. When time is precious, there's less time for team meetings and conflict resolution.

IT project managers face many challenges. However, effective IT project management can also bring a number of benefits to a company.

By overcoming the challenges of IT projects, you can ensure that more of your projects succeed.

Also, IT projects can enable you to improve your company's IT in many areas, such as security and information privacy.

Now that you understand the benefits of IT project management, consider this example of a company that decides to upgrade its project tracking software. The company puts together a team to address bugs in the software and improve its usability. Some managers find the tracking screen hard to follow.

Although the team members have other priorities, they know they have to complete the project within two months.

The project delivers an improved project tracking system that benefits all other projects in the company. Managers are better able to keep track of their projects and now find the system much more intuitive and easier to use.

Question

What are the benefits of IT project management?

Options:

1. More projects succeed
2. Improved IT security
3. Increased employee morale
4. Larger projects

Answer

Option 1: *This option is correct. By applying IT project management skills to your projects, you can ensure more of the projects succeed.*

Option 2: *This option is correct. IT project management can lead to improved IT security and enhanced data protection.*

Option 3: *This option is incorrect. On IT projects, there's rarely time to engage in traditional team-building exercises, which boost employee morale.*

Option 4: *This option is incorrect. Because the team members are usually on loan, IT projects tend to be shorter than other projects.*

4. Summary

Companies typically undertake many different types of projects, often at the same time. A project is any temporary undertaking that results in visible change. It has a definite beginning and end. All projects are unique undertakings that create a quality deliverable. They are made up of interdependent activities involving multiple resources.

Non-IT projects usually have a dedicated team with well-defined priorities. These projects can go on for months or years, but the technological risk remains constant. IT projects don't have dedicated teams. Team members often have conflicting priorities, so the projects rarely last longer than a few months. The technological risks often change as an IT project progresses.

Project management involves six key functions: initiating, planning, organizing, leading, controlling, and terminating. IT project management is used in projects where project success depends on some aspect of information technology. IT project management improves the success rate of projects, and leads to better IT security and information privacy.

IT PROJECT PHASES

1. 4 IT project phases

Being a project manager is a challenging but rewarding task. You must balance the often competing demands of managers, customers, and other stakeholders. You have to motivate and monitor your team. Your priorities can change suddenly. Unexpected risks and problems can knock your project off track. You rarely have enough time, money, or resources to get everything done. However, by carefully applying project management skills, you can bring even the most difficult projects to a successful conclusion.

You may feel overwhelmed when faced with a new project. There is so much to do and the deadlines often seem to be so tight.

To make them more manageable, projects are broken down into smaller chunks.

The overall project life cycle is broken down into phases, and each of these phases is broken down into processes. Project managers use processes to ensure that each phase of the project life cycle is completed correctly. Each process involves carrying out a series of tasks, such as designing a new network, assembling a new keyboard, or testing a new computer.

The project management processes are carried out during four main project life cycle phases. The names of these phases may vary from organization to organization. In this course, the first phase is called the Initiation phase, and the second is called the Planning phase. The Executing and Controlling phase is third, and the Closure phase is fourth.

Initiation

In the Initiation phase, the initiating processes are carried out. The project requirements, scope, and objectives are defined.

Planning

The Planning processes are carried out during the Planning phase. The project schedule and budget are defined, and the responsibilities of team members are clarified.

Executing and Controlling

During the Executing and Controlling phase, the Executing, and Monitoring and Controlling processes are completed. The new product or service is built and tested. This involves providing the necessary training, assembling the new product or service, monitoring its performance, and fixing any bugs.

Closure

The Closing processes are carried out during the Closure phase. The new product or service is delivered, all the necessary documentation is completed, and the lessons learned are noted.

Project phases must be carried out in the correct order. If a project jumps into the Executing and Controlling phase without properly completing the Planning phase, for example, the project team might not be adequately prepared for the project.

Projects tend to start off slowly during the Initiating and Planning phases. Peak activity occurs during the Executing and Controlling phase, and then work usually slows down again during the Closure phase.

To complete each phase, the project team must complete a number of activities.

First, each phase has a number of inputs. For example, a project charter is a necessary input for the Planning phase.

Each phase also has at least one concrete output. For example, the Planning phase delivers a work breakdown structure, or WBS. The WBS then becomes an input for the Executing and Controlling phase.

IT project managers can use a number of useful project management books to help them complete their tasks:

- the Project Management Body of Knowledge, or PMBOK, which outlines best project management prac-

tices
- the Software Engineering Body of Knowledge, or SWEBOK, which focuses on managing software engineering projects, and
- the Capability Maturity Model (Integrated), or CMMI, which explores best practices for deploying systems in an IT organization

Question

A project manager must ensure that the project phases are completed in sequence. Place the four project management phases in the correct order.

Options:

    A.   Initiation
    B.   Planning
    C.   Executing and Controlling
    D.   Closure

Answer

Correct answer(s):

In the first phase, Initiation, the project requirements, scope, and objectives are defined.

In the second phase, Planning, the project schedule and budget are defined.

In the third phase, Executing and Controlling, the new product is built, tested, and fixed as necessary.

In the fourth phase, Closure, the project is formally closed and the lessons learned are recorded.

2. The Initiation phase

The Initiation phase is when the idea for the project is first explored. The project manager and other project stakeholders gather all the necessary data about the proposed project. They then have to decide whether to proceed with the project.

For a project to succeed, it must meet a specific need. The project manager has to consult with the potential customers to ensure that everyone agrees what the specific IT needs are.

For example, an organization might take on a contract to develop and program a back office inventory software system for a large chain of office equipment suppliers.

Once you understand the client's needs, you need to set objectives. The project manager must also define the project objectives. Project objectives must always be "SMART." In other words, they should be specific, measurable, attainable, realistic, and time-bound.

Question

Which of these objectives do you think is a good IT project objective?

Options:

1. Improve broadband availability in the office for all employees
2. To ensure wireless broadband speeds of three megabits per second are available to all employees by the end of the year
3. To put in place a new wireless broadband infrastructure with fast speeds by the end of the week

Answer

Option 1: *This option is incorrect. This objective is too vague and it isn't time-bound.*

Option 2: *This is the correct option. This objective is specific, measurable, attainable, realistic, and time-bound.*

Option 3: *This option is incorrect. This objective doesn't define how fast the broadband has to be. Also, the target of completing the project by the end of the week is unlikely to be realistic.*

Before starting to build a new IT product, an organization must ensure that it has the resources necessary to build it. This includes making sure that it has the skills, budget, and time required.

By conducting a feasibility analysis, the project manager can ensure whether the organization can successfully complete the project.

When developing a new IT product, the project team must know exactly what's expected of it. Every project must have a clearly defined scope.

The team must have a clear idea of what features and functionality have to be incorporated into the product, and what can be left out.

The project manager must ensure that the team members have the IT skill sets required to complete the project.

In some cases, the manager may need to recruit IT experts specifically to work on the projects. In other cases, existing employees have to be trained in new skills.

The main output from the Initiation phase is the project charter. This is the official authorization for the project. It typically signals the organization's commitment to the project and outlines the business reasons for the project and its preliminary scope.

Question

What are the key activities in the Initiation phase?

Options:

1. Define the limits of the project
2. Decide what the project needs to achieve
3. Ensure the feasibility of the project
4. Outline the business reasons for the project
5. Create the project schedule
6. Finalize the project budget

Answer

Option 1: *This option is correct. The project scope outlines what the project is expected to achieve and what's beyond its limits.*

Option 2: *This option is correct. Once you understand the client's needs, you can establish project objectives. Project objectives should be specific, measurable, attainable, realistic, and time-bound.*

Option 3: *This option is correct. The feasibility study checks whether the project meets a clear business need and whether the organization has the resources to complete the project successfully.*

Option 4: *This option is correct. The project charter is the formal authorization to proceed with the project. It outlines the business*

reasons for the project, along with the project scope.
Option 5: *This option is incorrect. It's still too early to create the project schedule.*
Option 6: *This option is incorrect. Although the feasibility study explores the budget needed for the project, the budget isn't finalized at this stage.*

3. The Planning phase

In the Planning phase, the ideas from the Initiation phase are refined into action plans, which together make up the project management plan. An effective Planning phase can help prevent problems from arising later in the project.

One of the key planning documents is the work breakdown structure, or WBS. It outlines all the tasks that have to be carried out in order to complete the project.

As the project progresses, new tasks might have to be added to the WBS. For example, more comprehensive testing may be needed to deal with unexpected software bugs.

The project manager can use the WBS in order to justify budget and schedule projections and requests for additional work.

It's sometimes useful to convert the tasks listed in the WBS into a flowchart. This enables the project manager to easily determine the order that the tasks have to be completed in.

Question

Which statements about the WBS are true?

Options:

1. It outlines the most important tasks in the project
2. It's used to create the project schedule
3. It can't be adjusted after the Planning phase
4. It can form part of the budget planning process

Answer

Option 1: *This option is incorrect. The WBS outlines all the tasks in the project, not just the most important ones.*
Option 2: *This option is correct. The WBS can be used to form the basis of the project schedule.*
Option 3: *This option is incorrect. The WBS can be updated as new*

tasks are added to the project.

Option 4: *This option is correct. The WBS can be used by the project manager in order to identify the resources needed and the budget for the project.*

Once the WBS is prepared, the project manager can then put together a schedule to complete the project tasks. In order to create a realistic schedule, the project manager must be confident that the information in the WBS is correct.

The schedule also outlines the development processes that will be used for the project. This enables the project manager to determine the most efficient way to complete the tasks in the time allowed.

The project manager can now start identifying the resources needed for the project. To do so, the project manager must also have a good idea of the IT product requirements, and make sure that these align with the WBS and the resources available.

In order to create an accurate budget, you, as the project manager, must make realistic projections of the project costs. The tighter the schedule, for example, the more resources will be needed and the higher the costs will be.

The preliminary product design is also completed during the Planning phase. Once all the stakeholders agree to this design, product development can begin and the project management plan can be created.

The project management plan is one of the key outputs from this phase. It outlines the project manager's understanding of the project and of how the project will accomplish its goals. The plan can form the basis of the project kickoff meeting, which is part of the next project phase.

Question

What are the key activities of the Planning phase?

Options:

1. Creating a plan for the project
2. Breaking the project down into tasks
3. Creating a schedule for the tasks

4. Developing the product
5. Working out the project costs
6. Rewriting the project charter

Answer

Option 1: *This option is correct. The project management plan outlines the project manager's understanding of the project and of how the project will accomplish its goals. It incorporates budget, scope, risk, and schedule planning, among other areas.*

Option 2: *This option is correct. The WBS outlines the tasks that have to be completed in order to meet the project objectives.*

Option 3: *This option is correct. The project schedule may comprise a master schedule and individual schedules for each phase or activity.*

Option 4: *This option is incorrect. The product is designed during the Planning phase, but it isn't developed.*

Option 5: *This option is correct. Once the project manager knows what resources are needed, work on the project budget can begin.*

Option 6: *This option is incorrect. Although the project charter may be altered during the Planning phase, it shouldn't be completely rewritten.*

4. The Executing and Controlling phase

During the Executing and Controlling phase, the new IT product or service is developed and tested, based on the designs that were created during the Planning phase. In IT projects, this phase is sometimes called the Implementation or Construction phase.

One of the main aims of the Executing and Controlling phase is to deliver a product based on the design specifications that were outlined in the Planning phase. A project manager can use a process map to ensure that all the tasks and procedures are in place, and that the product can be built according to specifications.

In order to complete the project, the project manager has to assemble a project team. A key project management responsibility is making sure that the team members have the IT skills necessary to carry out the project tasks.

The team must be managed on a day-to-day basis. This involves making sure they're meeting their objectives, addressing any problems they raise, providing them with direction and focus, and motivating them.

To help keep them focused on the project objectives, the project manager should hold regular project meetings with the team.

The project kickoff meeting is a particularly important meeting. It may be the first time all the team members have met, so it's an ideal opportunity for everyone to introduce themselves.

Project management during the Executing and Controlling phase is often a combination of directing, monitoring, and controlling.

Directing

Directing the project involves providing leadership for the project team. The project manager is responsible for communicating the project objectives to the team and making sure everyone has the resources needed to carry out their tasks.

For example, an IT project manager might feel that his team doesn't appreciate how important it is to release a new software package by the end of the financial quarter. So he calls a team meeting to reiterate the central role the new product will play in the company's marketing strategy in the next quarter.

Monitoring

A project manager monitors a project in order to check that it's meeting its objectives and targets. By carefully monitoring project progress, the project manager will be able to see immediately if a project is beginning to go over budget or fall behind schedule.

For example, the IT project manager might notice that the design work on the new software package is starting to slip behind schedule. Because the project deadlines are so strict, he decides to add three more designers to the team to help get the design back on schedule.

Controlling

No matter how well you plan a project, unexpected problems nearly always occur. Good project managers aren't expected to be able to predict every problem. However, they are expected to be able to deal with any problems that arise. Controlling involves identifying problems that are occurring in the project and finding solutions to minimize their effect.

For example, the IT project manager notices that an unexpectedly high number of bugs are being found during the testing of the new software package, so he drafts some more programmers into the team in order to find effective fixes. He also negotiates with the organization's management to ensure that extra resources will be made available to carry out further testing.

Quality control is a key activity or task involved in the execution and control of a project. The project team is expected to deliver a high-quality IT product. Ensuring quality is a three-step process:

- in the quality planning stage, the project manager identifies which quality standards need to be defined for the project
- in the quality assurance stage, the project manager ensures that the necessary quality standards are defined and circulated to the team, and
- in the quality control stage, the project manager ensures that the team is meeting the quality standards

The key output from the Executing and Controlling phase is a finished IT product that's in line with the design specifications and customer expectations.

Question

What are the key activities in the Executing and Controlling phase?

Options:

1. Bring together a team to work on the project
2. Manufacture an IT product
3. Address issues that arise in the project
4. Develop a design plan
5. Update management on the project's outcome

Answer

Option 1: This option is correct. The project manager assembles and develops the project team during this phase.
Option 2: This option is correct. The finished IT product is the key output from the Executing and Controlling phase.
Option 3: This option is correct. The project manager must monitor the project and deal with any problems that arise.
Option 4: This option is incorrect. Developing a design plan occurs earlier in the life cycle of a project.
Option 5: This option is incorrect. The project isn't finished yet, so the manager can't yet know its final outcome.

5. The Closure phase

The Closure phase is the final phase in the IT project life cycle. This is when the project team delivers the new IT product and the project manager considers what lessons were learned during the project.

Two key audits have to be performed during the Closure phase:

- a technical audit, and
- a financial audit.

Technical audit

A technical audit is carried out to ensure that the new IT product meets the design specifications and functions correctly. The team carries out a number of functionality tests to ensure there are no bugs in the product. If the product meets customer expectations, the project has achieved its objectives.

Financial

A financial audit is carried out to ensure all project costs have been accounted for and invoices have been paid. This is also a chance for the project manager to compare the forecasted budget to the actual budget. If the project has run over budget, the project manager must be able to explain why.

nce the tests have been completed and bugs have been fixed, the new IT product can be deployed. This usually involves a formal release to end users, whether they're internal customers within the organization or external customers in the market.

Before formally closing the project, the project manager has to record the lessons learned. These identify problems that arose during the project, how these problems were addressed, and how they can be avoided on future projects.

At this stage, the project manager can now close the IT project.

Job Aid

IT Project Phase Activities

Purpose: *Use this job aid to review the activities carried out in the different IT project phases.*

Different activities are carried out in the various phases of an IT project.

Activities carried out in each IT project phase	
Phase	**Activities**
Initiation	Determine IT needs Conduct feasibility analysis Gather information Define objectives Determine scope Create project charter
Planning	Create WBS Create project schedule Determine resource needs Determine cost estimates Create preliminary design Create project management plan
Executing and Controlling	Form, develop, and manage project team Keep quality on track Direct, monitor, and control project Define processes and procedures
Closure	Conduct technical and financial audit

	Deploy the product Record the lessons learned

Question

What are the key activities in the Closure phase?

Options:

1. Check that the product functions properly
2. Roll the new product out to users
3. Identify what was learned during the project
4. Start a new project
5. Market the new product

Answer

Option 1: *This option is correct. The project manager must ensure that the necessary technical and financial audits have been completed. This includes running functionality tests.*

Option 2: *This option is correct. The new product is rolled out to end users – either internal customers in the organization or external customers in the market.*

Option 3: *This option is correct. Lessons learned include problems that arose during the project and the solutions that were found.*

Option 4: *This option is incorrect. Starting a new project takes place during the Initiation phase of the next project.*

Option 5: *This option is incorrect. The project manager isn't responsible for marketing the new product.*

Question

Various activities take place during the different phases of a project. Match each activity to the project phase it occurs in.

Options:

A.   Conduct a feasibility analysis and define objectives

B.   Create the work breakdown structure and the project management plan

C.   Develop the project team and direct and control the project

D.   Conducts audits and records lessons learned

Targets:

1. Initiation phase
2. Planning phase
3. Executing and Controlling
4. Closure

Answer

During this phase, the project manager conducts a feasibility analysis, defines objectives, and determines the project scope.

During this phase, the project manager creates the work breakdown structure and the project management plan, and develops the project schedule.

In this phase, the project manager develops the project team and directs, controls, and monitors the project.

In this phase, the project manager conducts financial and technical audits, and records the lessons learned.

6. Summary

Project managers break the project life cycle down into phases and processes. During the Initiation phase, the IT needs are determined and a feasibility study is conducted. After gathering the necessary data, the project manager defines the project objectives, project scope, and skills needed.

In the Planning phase, the resource needs and design specifications are defined. The project manager also puts a schedule, a budget, and development processes in place for the project.

In the Executing and Controlling phase, the project manager forms and develops the project team. The project must be directed, monitored, and controlled to ensure that it's meeting the objectives and quality standards.

In the Closure phase, the new product is deployed after the necessary audits have been completed. Then the project manager must note the lessons learned.

Follow-on Activity

Completing IT Project Phase Activities

Purpose: *Use this follow-on activity to note the IT project activities* *that have been completed in each phase of a past IT project at your company or organization.*

You should keep track of all the activities that have been completed during each phase of your IT project.

IT project phase activities completed		
Phase	**Activities needed**	**Activities completed**
Initiation	Define project scope	
	Establish project objectives	
	Conduct feasibility study	
	Create the project charter	
Planning	Create the project management plan	
	Create the WBS	
	Create the project schedule	
	Set the project budget	
Executing and Controlling	Assemble project team	
	Address project issues	
	Build IT product	
Closure	Check product functionality	
	Deploy product	

	Record lessons learned	

PROJECT MANAGEMENT TOOLS

1. Project management tools

As a project manager, you can use a number of basic project management tools to help you keep track of your project. These tools and techniques can be applied to any IT project, whether it involves hardware, services, software, or a combination of all three.

But although project management tools can be applied to any IT project, they're not always applied successfully.

IT projects have a number of characteristics that make them different from other projects. These include IT risk and the competitive landscape. If you don't take these characteristics into account, you may not correctly apply the tools to your IT project.

You can use several project management tools in your IT project:

- the work breakdown structure, or WBS, which breaks each project phase into a number of tasks
- network diagrams, which enable you to see the flow of work through a project
- Gantt charts, which provide a graphic representation of the project schedule, and
- earned value, which enables you to track the actual progress of your project

Question

Why are project management tools not always successfully applied in IT projects?

Options:

1. Project managers can sometimes fail to take into ac-

count the characteristics of IT projects
2. Project management tools are too basic for IT projects
3. Project management tools are useful only in IT projects involving hardware
4. IT projects don't have to be managed as closely as other projects

Answer

Option 1: *This is the correct option. Project managers must take into account characteristics such as IT risk and the competitive landscape.*

Option 2: *This option is incorrect. Basic IT tools can be applied to any project, including IT projects.*

Option 3: *This option is incorrect. Project management tools can be used in IT projects that involve hardware, software, services, or a combination of all three.*

Option 4: *This option is incorrect. IT projects use the same project management techniques as other projects.*

2. Work breakdown structure

The work breakdown structure, or **WBS**, breaks a project down into its individual tasks and activities. In order for the project to succeed, every item on the WBS must be completed. The WBS is a crucial tool for the project manager. A carefully thought out WBS can form the basis of a reliable project schedule and realistic budget. It also gives the project manager a good overview of the entire project.

The WBS is one of the major outputs from the Planning phase.

It's also an essential input into the Monitoring and Controlling phase because it helps the project manager keep track of the many tasks in the project.

If a task isn't listed on the WBS, it's outside the scope of the project.

The WBS breaks down project activities into different levels of detail. These levels can be displayed in an indented format, or they can be displayed in a graphical format.

Indented format

In the indented format, each level of the WBS is indented to the right. The lower the level, the further to the right it is indented. Individual tasks are usually the lowest level of the WBS, so these are indented the most to the right.

This WBS format tends to be very popular because most project management software applications support the indented format.

Graphical format

In the graphical format, the WBS is displayed like an organizational chart. Higher levels are displayed at the top of the chart, and low-level individual tasks are displayed at the bottom.

This format is particularly useful for project managers who like visual representations of the overall project. However, this format can result in large, complex graphics that not all project management software applications can display.

The WBS decomposes the project into levels.

This means that project activities are broken down into increasingly detailed levels.

A project is often decomposed into five levels:

- level 1, which is the highest level, and is usually just the project name
- level 2, which includes the major project sections and subsystems of the overall project
- level 3, which includes the major activities in each section of the project
- level 4, which includes the major tasks in each activity, and
- level 5, which includes each discrete task that has to be carried out

Not every IT project is decomposed down into five levels. Many projects have only four levels.

The lowest level in the WBS is the individual discrete task that can be assigned to a person. These individual tasks are known as work packages.

Consider how a project to build a new computer network would be decomposed into four levels:

- at level 1, the only item would be the overall project, which is to build a new computer system
- at level 2, the items would include the major project sections, such as building computers, laying down cables, and setting up connections
- at level 3, the items would include building components such as a computer motherboard, monitor, and keyboard, and
- at level 4, the items would include installing the central processing unit, the graphic, network, and memory cards, and fans

Question

Which of these statements is true about the role of the WBS in a project?

Options:

1. It's a major output from the Monitoring and Controlling phase
2. It divides a project into individual tasks
3. Every WBS in an IT project must have five levels
4. The graphical WBS is the most popular type

Answer

Option 1: *This option is incorrect. The WBS is a major output from the Planning phase and a major input into the Monitoring and Controlling phase.*

Option 2: *This is the correct option. The WBS breaks projects down into increasingly detailed activities and tasks.*

Option 3: *This option is incorrect. Many IT projects require only four levels.*

Option 4: *This option is incorrect. The indented WBS is typically the most popular type. Some IT project management software applications can't handle the graphical WBS format.*

3. Network diagrams

Network diagrams are another project management tool. They're usually developed during the Planning phase, and are used to plot the flow of work from the beginning of the project until the end. As well as outlining what project tasks must be completed, they estimate the duration of each task. Using this information, the project manager can then develop the project schedule.

The WBS enables you to see at a glance what tasks must be carried out in order for you to complete your project. It arranges the tasks into logical groupings.

The network diagram enables you to determine what order the tasks should be carried out in. It arranges the tasks in sequence.

The information in the network diagrams forms the basis of the project schedule.

The network diagram provides estimates for the duration of each task. These estimates are based on previous experience and resource availability.

When estimating the duration for each task, it's best not to plan for either the worst-case scenario or the best-case scenario. Take into account likely risks and make a realistic estimate.

As well as understanding the sequence of the tasks, project managers need to appreciate the interactions between the tasks. These interactions usually take the form of dependencies, relationships, and constraints.

Dependencies

Dependencies between tasks can be mandatory or discretionary. A mandatory dependency occurs when tasks must be carried out in a certain order. For example, you cannot connect your computers until you've laid down the network cables.

A discretionary dependency occurs when it's preferable to carry out tasks in certain order. For example, it's preferable to complete all testing before rolling out a new software system.

Relationships

The most common relationship is a finish-to-start dependency. This means that one task cannot start until another task is complete. For example, you cannot test a software application until the application has been built.

A finish-to-finish relationship occurs when two tasks must finish at the same time. When two tasks have to start at the same time, it's known as a start-to-start relationship. The fourth type of relationship is a start-to-finish relationship, which occurs when one task can't finish until another one has started.

Constraints

Constraints are anything that could prevent the project work flow from being completed as expected. For example, the project work flow is usually based on the assumption that a certain number of resources will be available. If you don't have enough programmers on your project, your ability to successfully complete the project will be constrained.

Network diagrams enable project managers to see at a glance how work should flow through a project.

Ensuring that the project work flows as expected is one of the key tasks in the Monitoring and Controlling phase of any IT project.

Question

How are network diagrams used in project management?

Options:

1. Network diagrams show the best-case duration of each task
2. Network diagrams show how work should flow through a project
3. Network diagrams show dependencies and constraints
4. Network diagrams are developed during the Initiation phase

Answer

Option 1: This option is incorrect. Network diagrams use estimated durations that usually fall between the best-case and worst-case scenarios.

Option 2: *This option is correct. During the Monitoring and Controlling phase, the project manager tries to ensure that project work flow is aligned with the network diagram.*

Option 3: *This option is correct. Network diagrams show the interactions between tasks, such as relationships, constraints, and dependencies.*

Option 4: *This option is incorrect. Network diagrams are developed during the Planning phase.*

4. Gantt charts

The WBS can be used to break a project down into logically grouped tasks, and the network diagram shows the best sequence for completing the tasks. However, both these tools are based on the estimated progression of the project. Another tool, the **Gantt chart**, enables the project manager to compare estimated progress with actual project progress.

Using information from the WBS and the network diagram, the project manager can create a project schedule, based on estimates of how long each task will take to complete.

The Gantt chart is essentially a graphic version of the project schedule. It shows how the project should be progressing, according to the schedule.

And it also shows how the project is actually progressing. This enables the project manager to see immediately whether the project is on schedule.

To create a Gantt chart, you have to add a number of elements:
- the task list
- the timeline
- the estimated completion dates, and
- the actual completion dates

Task list

The task list outlines all the tasks that have to be carried out in order to complete the project. This information is taken from the WBS.

Timeline

The timeline shows the estimated duration for the entire project. It's based on the total durations in the network diagram.

Estimated completion dates

The estimated completion dates are based on the information in the project schedule. And the schedule is based on the durations estimated in the network diagram.

Actual completion dates

The actual completion dates show when each task was completed. The project manager can then see whether the project has started to fall behind schedule.

Gantt charts are very effective tracking tools because they show how the project is progressing in a simple manner.

They are also useful communication tools because they highlight areas where projects are falling behind schedule. This indicates which aspects of the project are experiencing problems.

Question

What do Gantt charts aim to identify?

Options:

1. The estimated duration of the project
2. The actual progress of the project
3. The problems that are arising in the project
4. The tasks that must be completed in the project
5. Whom the tasks are assigned to

Answer

Option 1: This option is correct. Gantt charts use the duration information in the network diagram to show the estimated duration of the project.

Option 2: This option is correct. Gantt charts indicate when each task was completed and compare this to when it should have been completed.

Option 3: This option is incorrect. Gantt charts can indicate where there are problems in the project, but they don't identify what the problems are.

Option 4: This option is correct. Gantt charts list all the tasks identi-

fied in the WBS.

Option 5: *This option is incorrect. Gantt charts show what the project tasks are, but they don't specify whom the tasks are assigned to.*

5. Earned value analysis

The WBS shows the project manager the tasks that have to be completed in the project. He then uses this information to forecast the schedule. The Gantt chart shows him the actual progress compared to forecasted progress. This also enables him to calculate what percentage of the project has been completed. Another tool he can use is **earned value analysis**.

The earned value is the amount of the project budget that has been used up at a particular time in a project. In order to calculate the earned value, the project manager has to know the planned valued, the actual cost, and the work performed.

Planned value

The planned value, or PV, is the estimated budget. The project manager can add up the PV for each particular task in order to get the total PV for the project.

The PV represents what the project manager thinks the project is going to cost.

Actual cost

The actual cost, or AC, is how much the project actually costs. As a project progresses and more tasks are completed, the AC increases.

By comparing PV with AC, the project manager can get a good indication whether the project is going over budget. However, in order to get a proper sense of whether the project is on budget, the project manager must also take into account the work completed at any point in the project.

Work performed

The work performed enables the project manager to see how much of the budget has been spent at a particular time in a project and compare this with what should have been spent at that point.

Suppose a project is expected to cost $100,000 and the costs build up in a linear fashion throughout the project.

Assume that the project is on schedule. When the project is 30% completed, the project manager would expect that the project has cost $30,000 so far. That means that 30% of the work has been completed and 30% of the budget has been used up. The earned value of the project at that point is $30,000.

However, suppose the project has fallen behind schedule. Say only 25% of the project was completed when the project manager expected 30% to be completed. At that point, the PV would be $30,000, but the earned value would only be 25% of the budget, or $25,000.

Using the earned value figure, the project manager can calculate a number of measurements. These include the cost and schedule variance, the schedule and cost performance indexes, the estimates at completion, and the estimate to complete.

Cost and schedule variance

The cost variance is the difference between the earned value and the actual cost at a particular point in the project. If the earned value is higher than the actual cost, the project is under budget.

The schedule variance is the difference between the earned value and the planned value at a particular point in a project. If the earned value is higher than the planned value, the project is ahead of schedule.

Schedule and cost performance indexes

The schedule performance index divides the earned value by the planned value. If this value is higher than 1, the project is ahead of schedule.

The cost performance index divides the earned value by the actual cost. If this value is higher than 1, the project is under budget.

Estimates at completion

Schedule estimates often have to be revised as a project progresses. In order to calculate the new completion date, the project manager can divide the original completion estimate by the schedule performance index. For example, if the original estimate for the project was 100 days, and the schedule performance index is 0.8, then the new estimated project duration is 125 days.

Similarly, budget estimates are also revised during a project. By dividing the original budget estimate by the cost performance index, the project manager can work out the new budget estimate. For example, if the project budget is $10,000 and the cost performance index is 1.25, then the new budget estimate is $8,000.

Estimate to complete

The estimate to complete value helps the project manager work out how much money is required to take a project from a particular point to the end of the project. This alerts the project manager if he needs to ask for more money for the project. By subtracting the actual cost from the updated budget estimate at completion, the project manager knows how much money is required to complete the project.

Earned value analysis uses mathematical techniques to help the project manager judge whether a project is on schedule and still operating within budget.

Question

Which of these statements are true about the role of earned value in IT projects?

Options:

1. It uses graphics to track project progress
2. It compares the estimated costs with the actual project costs
3. It helps the project manager update the project budget estimate as necessary
4. It enables the project manager to assign resources more effectively

Answer

Option 1: *This option is incorrect. Earned value analysis uses mathematical techniques instead of graphics to track project progress.*

Option 2: *This option is correct. Earned value analysis involves comparing estimated schedules and budgets with actual project performance.*

Option 3: *This option is correct. Earned value analysis enables the project manager to update estimates at completion.*

Option 4: *This option is incorrect. Earned value analysis tracks project performance rather than resource allocation.*

Question

Match each project management tool to its description.

Options:

A.	WBS
B.	Network diagrams
C.	Gantt charts
D.	Earned value

Targets:

1. This tool decomposes a project into increasingly detailed activities and tasks
2. This tool shows the best sequence for project tasks to be completed in
3. This tool provides a graphical representation to compare predicted project progress with actual progress
4. This tool uses mathematical techniques to compare the budget forecast to the actual project costs

Answer

The WBS decomposes project activities into increasingly detailed activities and tasks by breaking them down into four or five levels.

Network diagrams show the best sequence for project tasks to be completed in and the estimated duration for each task.

Gantt charts provide a graphical representation to compare predicted project progress with actual progress. They enable the project manager to see at a glance whether the project is on schedule.

Earned value analysis uses mathematical techniques to compare the budget forecast to the actual project costs. It also compares the esti-mated schedule with the actual schedule.

6. Summary

Project managers can use a number of project management tools to help them manage IT projects. However, they have to remember the unique characteristics of IT projects when using these tools.

The work breakdown structure, or WBS, breaks a project down into individual tasks. Network diagrams show the preferred flow of work through a project. Gantt charts enable project managers to compare forecasted project progress with actual project progress. And earned valued analysis uses mathematical techniques to track project progress.

Job Aid

Using Project Management Tools

Purpose: *Use this job aid to review when and why you would use the different project management tools.*

You use different project management tools at different stages in your IT projects.

Using project management tools	
Tool	**When and why**
Work breakdown structure (WBS)	You use the WBS at the start of the project to break the project down into individual tasks and group these tasks logically
Network diagram	You use the network diagram at the start of the project to chart how the work should flow through the project and estimate how long each task will take to complete
Gantt chart	You use the Gantt chart when the project is up and running to monitor project progress
Earned value	You use earned value analysis when the

analysis	project is up and running to compare budget forecasts with actual costs, and compare estimated progress with actual progress

IT PROJECT MANAGEMENT ESSENTIALS: INITIATING AND PLANNING IT PROJECTS

Good managers are usually familiar with the saying that a good start is half the job done. This applies to every project, and to IT projects in particular. If you want your IT projects to succeed, don't underestimate the early stages of the process – the initiation and planning phases. The initiation phase is about clarifying the project goals and requirements. The planning phase is about working out what needs to be done, when it needs to be done, and how much it's likely to cost.

There are two key reasons why you need to pay attention to these phases. First, if you don't know what you're aiming for, you're unlikely to hit the target. And second, if you haven't carefully considered the work to be done and the resources needed, you're likely to run into trouble sooner or later. It can be tempting to ignore the initiation and planning phases because they seem to delay the project, but they'll save you time and money in the end.

This course describes the basics of initiating and planning an IT project:

- you'll learn about some methods for defining the nature and scope of your project from the start
- you'll be introduced to the work breakdown structure, which breaks down the project deliverables into all the tasks that must be done to complete a project

  A project to install upgrades at two sites breaks down into installation of upgrades and user training. The installation further breaks down into installing at Sites A and B. The training breaks down into two components: develop training and deliver training. The latter breaks down into deliver training at Site A, and deliver training at Site B.
- you'll learn about the techniques for sequencing tasks and scheduling for maximum efficiency in completing the project, and
- you'll find out about different techniques for estimating project costs

This course will provide you with important foundational knowledge about initiating and planning IT projects. This will make you more effective as an IT project manager and make it more likely that your projects will succeed and benefit your organization.

Initiating and Planning IT Projects
1. Initiating an IT Project
2. Developing a WBS for an IT Project
3. Schedule Planning for an IT Project
4. Cost Planning for an IT project

INITIATING AN IT PROJECT

1. Define the problem

Imagine your boss presents you with the opportunity to manage a new IT project. Rather than rushing headlong into the project, your first step is to clarify what the project involves. This is the initiation phase of project management. And it's vital you don't underestimate its importance. Good analysis and clarification of client requirements from the start can save countless hours and change requests later. Many IT projects that fail do so because the initiation phase has been neglected.

To start with, you should be clear about the **source of the project**. Is it based on some felt need that emerged within the organization? Or has it come down from upper management?

Needs-driven projects sometimes stem from compatibility issues. For example, part of an internal application may need to be rewritten to provide more seamless integration with a financial software package.

Assigned projects typically come down from upper management to address a particular want on behalf of the organization or an external customer request. For example, an executive might want to capitalize on a unique opportunity in the market. Alternatively, there are **handed-on projects**. In these cases, you are appointed to manage a project that is already partially planned – one that was previously put on hold.

But whatever the origins of your IT project, your project management role now enters a data-gathering phase.

Your first job in this phase is to go back to the project request and take steps to clarify the request as much as possible. Business analysts or technical experts may be able to help you in this task. If you have been involved in the initiation phase of a project, you may have followed four steps that are typically taken to clarify project requests. The first of these steps is to define the problem that gave rise to the request. Another step is to identify client requirements. In addition, you should conduct a feasibility study and describe product and project scope.

There are good reasons for the first step – defining the problem from the start. Have you ever been on a project where people were scrambling to meet deadlines but where no one seemed to know the reason for the work? And then suddenly the project gets completely changed or abandoned? If you've been in this situation, it's probably because the problem that gave rise to the project wasn't clearly defined from the start.

As the project manager, your first job is to determine exactly what the client means by the request. You may have to further define the purpose of the client request because details may be vague.

For example, if you're asked to produce a user manual for an application, you need to clarify which format the manual should be in.

Or suppose you get a request for "a computerized customer relationship management system to improve the quality and efficiency of customer care." This fails to clarify how the system will be used to improve customer care. Not only that, it doesn't specify what improving customer care means.

Once you've investigated the request, it's a good idea to communicate in writing your understanding of the request to the client to prevent any future misunderstanding. This will serve as a project concept document.

Another reason it's worth clarifying requests is that they are often presented in the form of solutions. The earlier example of the request for a computerized customer relationship management system to improve customer care illustrates this. The system is supposed to be a solution to a customer care problem.

But is the solution correct? Unfortunately, as a project manager, you can't assume that it is. So you must identify the problem before considering the solution.

Question

Which statements illustrate reasons for defining the problem that gave rise to a project request?

Options:

1. The request may be presented as a solution
2. The wording of the request may be vague
3. Lack of clarity about the problem may cause a project to fail
4. Defining the problem helps you reword it as a action-focused solution
5. You won't have to write a project concept document

Answer

Option 1: This is a correct option. Sometimes requests are presented as the solution to a problem, but the project manager can't assume the solution is correct. The problem must be articulated before considering the solution.

Option 2: This is a correct option. If a request is not specific enough, the product may not meet the client's requirements.

Option 3: This is a correct option. A project may have to be abandoned later because there was a lack of clarity about its purpose at the beginning.

Option 4: This is not a correct option. At this early stage of the project life cycle, the project manager is only interested in defining the problem, not in proposing solutions.

Option 5: This is not a correct option. Defining the problem should lead to a project concept document rather than enable you to avoid having to write one.

2. IDENTIFY CLIENT'S REQUIREMENTS

Once you're clear about the problem or need that generated the request, the next step is to clarify what your client's requirements, objectives, and expectations for the project outcome are. You need to consider functional requirements, business requirements, and technical requirements.

Functional requirements focus on how the end user will interact with the product. For example, an electronic information provider might require that customers of the database have free text searchability and full-text access.

As always, you need to ensure that the requirements are clear and unambiguous. If a requirement is that customers will find the database easy to use, you need to know exactly what that entails. Does it refer to the flow of the screens, the built-in help, or other aspects?

Next you should consider the organization's **business requirements**. As project manager, you need to know why the company wants to invest in the project – for example, is it to generate revenue, reduce costs, or comply with regulations?

Finally, you should understand the **technical requirements** involved. These are the product characteristics that are needed so that the product can perform the functional requirements. Examples of technical requirements might be that the system response time can't be more than ten seconds or that the system should be able to run on multiple operating systems.

In addition to the requirements mentioned already, there are **constraints** that frame how a project has to be managed. For instance, the project deliverable may have to be completed by a certain date. In this case, the schedule represents a constraint. It may compel you to hire additional personnel to complete the project on time.

Other examples of constraints are cost and quality level.

Project requirements aren't just important – they're the project's reason for existence. So it's vital to explicitly document what these requirements are. A clearly written set of requirements helps ensure that you're on the same page as the client when it comes to what the outcome of the project is supposed to be.

The project requirements document should contain clearly defined high-level requirements with measurable objectives and good supporting data regarding strategic value and timing.

The document will also have any relevant historical data on similar projects. A high-level requirements document is critical to project approval, as well as to ongoing communications regarding the project.

Question

Match each type of requirement to the example of that requirement.

Options:

    A.   Functional

    B.   Business

    C.   Technical

Targets:

    1. Customers can access their accounts online
    2. The project should increase the organization's revenue stream
    3. The application must be compatible with the latest version of the company's operating system

Answer

Functional requirements specify how end users can interact with the product.

Projects are meant to contribute to general business objectives. Increasing revenue would be one such objective.

Technical requirements are characteristics the product requires so that it can achieve the necessary functionality.

3. Conduct a feasibility study

Another way to clarify a project request is to conduct a feasibility study. The main purpose of this is to investigate whether the organization has sufficient resources and expertise to carry out the project. Unfortunately, organizations may fail to do a study, and then proceed with projects without confirming they have the resources or technical capability to carry out the project. Many IT projects collapse because no feasibility study was conducted at the outset.

The feasibility study is usually conducted with the help of a business analyst and supporting team members, and is overseen by the project manager. It typically includes financial projections; a general description of the business; details on the management of the project; statements about the competition; and a cash-flow projection based on averages. Cost benefit analysis and calculations of net present value and return on investment are also part of assessing feasibility.

As noted, the feasibility study determines whether the company has the technical and resource capabilities to do the project. But it serves other purposes too.

It answers the question of the project's strategic value. Will the project contribute to the company's long-term growth plans?

The feasibility analysis may indicate that the project fits the company's strategic goals but that the company doesn't have the ability to complete it. In that case, the company may decide to hire additional team members or pool resources with another company.

Question

Which statements accurately express purposes of a feasibility study?

Options:

      1. Helps decide if the company's resources are adequate for the project

2. Answers the question of whether the project would contribute to the company's overall strategy
3. Determines what the functional requirements for the product are
4. Clarifies the problem the project is meant to solve

Answer

Option 1: *This is a correct option. The feasibility study considers whether the company's technical and other resource capabilities match the resource requirements of the project.*

Option 2: *This is a correct option. The feasibility study includes statements about whether the project fits into the company's strategic plan.*

Option 3: *This is not a correct option. Identifying client requirements is a separate step in the initiation phase.*

Option 4: *This is not a correct option. Defining the problem comes before a feasibility study in the initiation phase of a project.*

4. Describe project and product scope

In addition to defining the problem, identifying and documenting client requirements, and completing a well-researched feasibility analysis, you should describe the product scope and the project scope.

First consider the **product scope**. This emphasizes defining the functions and characteristics of the product. For example, how big, what color, how responsive, and how reliable should it be? The point is just to identify these desirables. The technical methods of how to achieve them come later, with the development of the systems architecture.

Project scope, on the other hand, comprises all the activities required to support developing the product, service, or result. It may be defined as all the work that needs to be done to deliver the project's objectives. Work here is not broken down in detail, but simply described generally.

In describing project scope, you ignore the time and cost involved in carrying out the project.

Describing project scope is important because differing perceptions about scope can cause serious problems down the line. For example, perhaps the project manager assumed that the new system would be able to generate four types of reports, but the client assumed there would also be two additional kinds of reports. So it's crucial that there's a common understanding of project scope.

The end product of the initiation planning process is a project charter. The charter is the project blueprint, like the blueprint you develop if you build a new home. The finished product will look very different, but at least you now have a map to help you get started.

The charter describes the project, specifies the project team needed, sets out goals and objectives, and makes a business case for the project.

Project charters are often viewed as the official start of the project, authorizing it and allowing the project manager to apply the necessary resources.

Job Aid
Steps to Take When Initiating an IT Project
Purpose: *Use this job aid to review steps to take when initiating an IT project.*

Table 1: Steps involved in initiating an IT project	
Step to use in initiating a project	**Actions typical for each step**
Define the problem	Make sure the problem or need that generated the project request is clearly defined and understood. Investigate the request and communicate your understanding of it. Identify the problem prior to proposing a solution.
Identify the client's requirements	Understand what the client's expectations, requirements, and objectives for the project outcome are. Consider functional, business,

	and technical requirements. Consider constraints on the project. Create a document that includes a statement of the problem, the objectives, the strategic value, the requirements, and the timing.
Conduct a feasibility analysis	Provide notes on financial projections; a general description of the business; an account of how the project will be formed, managed, and marketed; statements concerning the competition; and a cash-flow projection based on averages. Consider whether the project will work and whether the company has the resources and expertise to carry it out. Consider whether the project is compatible with the company's strategic plan.
Describe project and product scope	Define the boundaries of the product. Begin to create a work breakdown structure.

Question

Match steps associated with clarifying a project request to examples of how they're carried out.

Options:

    A.   Define the problem
    B.   Identify the client's requirements
    C.   Conduct a feasibility analysis
    D.   Describe the project and product scope

Targets:

    1. Clarify what gave rise to a project request before proposing a solution
    2. Find out why the company wants to invest in this project, as well as the functional and technical specifications needed

3. Consider if the company has the resources to under-take the project
4. Determine the work that needs to be done to achieve the project's goal

Answer

In some cases, problems of definition arise because the project manager is presented with a request that's meant to solve a problem. It's important that the project manager determine what the problem is because what's proposed may not really be a solution.

The project manager needs to know what the project is meant to achieve for the client. One aspect of this is the business reason for the project. Moreover, it's important to figure out the technical and functional requirements for the project outcome.

A feasibility study has to determine whether the organization has the resources or technical capability to meet the client's needs.

This expresses the meaning of project scope. It describes the work needed in general, not in detail, as distinct from the costs or time required to carry out the project.

5. Summary

The initiation phase of any IT project is crucial. It's where the nature and scope of the project and the client's requirements get clarified. Failure to achieve this clarification at an early stage can lead to problems and even to abandoning the project down the line.

Four steps are recommended during this phase. One of these steps is to define the problem that gave rise to the request for the project. Another is to identify the client's functional, business, and technical requirements. A third step is to conduct a feasibility study, which examines whether the company has the resources and expertise to carry the project through. Finally, it's important to describe the product and project scope.

Follow-on Activity

Identifying Steps Taken in Initiating a Project

Purpose: *Use this follow-on activity to reflect on the steps you took* *in the last IT project you initiated.*

Recall the initiation phase of the last IT project you worked on. Reflect on the actions you took in relation to the steps discussed in the topic.

Table 1: Identifying steps taken in the initiation phase of an IT project		
Recommended steps when initiating a project	**What actions did you take?**	**What would you do differently next time?**
Define the problem		
Identify the client's requirements		
Conduct a feasibility study		
Describe product and project scope		

DEVELOPING A WBS FOR AN IT PROJECT

1. Scope planning

When a project charter is approved, it's time for project planning to begin. Planning can be one of the most overlooked areas of project management. You may even have been rebuked for wasting valuable time planning when there was work to be done. But a good understanding of the planning process will prepare you to convince your organization of the benefits of taking the time up front to define all aspects of a project before the work actually begins.

Project planning begins by clarifying the project's scope with the help of the project charter that emerged from the initiation process. Project scope is the extent of the work involved in completing the project. As a project manager, you need to know the boundaries of the project – what is part of it and what is not. The scope planning process leads to a scope statement, a scope management plan, and a work breakdown structure, or WBS.

The scope statement provides a common understanding of the project by documenting the project objectives and deliverables. This statement is the basis for many of the other planning processes. It's also the basis for setting the boundaries of the project with the client and stakeholders. It should include a project justification, a project description, and the major deliverables. The scope statement should also detail time and cost estimates, success criteria, assumptions, and constraints.

The scope management plan documents the procedures you'll use to manage any proposed changes to the project scope throughout the life of the project.

The final component of scope is the work breakdown structure – the WBS. This takes the major deliverables from the scope statement and subdivides them into smaller, more manageable components from which you can estimate task durations, assign resources, and estimate costs.

It's the WBS that forms the basis for cost and schedule estimates.

Question

Which documents get created during the scope planning process?

Options:

1. Work breakdown structure
2. Scope statement
3. Project charter
4. Scope management plan
5. Requirements document

Answer

Option 1: This is a correct option. The work breakdown structure (WBS) breaks down project deliverables into smaller components from which you can estimate task durations, assign resources, and estimate costs.

Option 2: This is a correct option. The scope statement document should describe project justification, project description, major deliverables, success criteria, assumptions, constraints, and estimates of how long the project will take and how much it will cost.

Option 3: This option is incorrect. The project charter should be approved at the end of the initiation phase of project management. This is before the planning process gets underway.

Option 4: This is a correct option. The scope management plan documents which procedures will be used to manage any proposed changes to the project scope throughout the life of the project.

Option 5: This option is incorrect. Documenting client requirements is part of the initiation phase that should already have taken place before scope planning begins.

2. The work breakdown structure (WBS)

More needs to be said about the final element of scope planning, the WBS. The WBS is a really important project management tool. It breaks down the project into manageable and achievable chunks. It gives a clear view of all the work that needs to go into the project. And it forms the basis for time estimates, cost estimates, and resource assignments. A standard way of representing the WBS is by an organizational, or hierarchical tree chart.

Typically, a WBS has five levels. The top level is the project title. The next level down itemizes the major project subsystems. The third level identifies the major deliverables into which the project can be divided. Next, there's a level of subdeliverables. Finally, the subdeliverables are broken down into specific work packages. Each level is more detailed than the one above it, but the totals of each level should be equivalent.

As a last step, it's important to assign numeric indicators to each level to keep track of the work. For example, if the project itself is labeled 1.0, the second major subsystem is 1.2, the first deliverable for that subsystem is 1.2.1, and so on.

Project name
This is the most general level. It encompasses the whole project as articulated in all the tasks on the levels below it.

Project subsystems
These might be phases corresponding to the project life cycle – initiation, planning, execution, closing – or they might refer to the specific kinds of requirements identified in the scope statement – business, functional, and technical requirements. They are sometimes referred to as subprojects and are typically the major areas of work for a project.

Major deliverables
Deliverables are goals, products, or services that must be delivered before the project can be considered complete. Each subsystem of the project will have key deliverables associated with it.

Subdeliverables
Subdeliverables are tasks into which the major deliverables can

be divided. Subdeliverables must be finished before the major deliverable is considered complete.

Work packages

The work package is the minimum unit in a WBS. Work packages are activities or tasks that can be easily assigned and estimated, and produce a meaningful deliverable. As a rule of thumb, these should not require less than 8 hours or more than 80 hours of work to complete.

So the WBS breaks your complex project into interrelated discrete tasks, using a hierarchical tree structure. Put another way, the WBS is about organizing your project into logical groupings. For example, if your project is to create a new application, you'll have to design the application, develop the application, and then test it. These are the project's three major areas.

But to design the application, you need to have a design plan, which must include a physical design and a logical design. These can be called the major deliverables within the design branch of the project.

Consider a more detailed example. Suppose your project involves installing upgrades to 200 computer systems over two sites. The major subprojects are the installation of the upgrades, training of users, and management of the project. The installation area of the project can be subdivided into two deliverables: installations at Site A and Site B.

The training area is divided into four deliverables: define user training requirements, develop training, deliver training, and test. These may be further broken down into subdeliverables.

For example, defining user training requirements may involve two subdeliverables: identifying subject matter experts and interviewing them to establish appropriate content requirements. Delivery will have to be split into Site A and Site B.

Question

How would you place the components of a software development project in a WBS?

Match the selected components of such a project to their appropriate levels in the WBS.

Options:
- A. Execution phase
- B. Design tests
- C. Design manual tests
- D. Execute manual tests

Targets:
1. Project subsystem
2. Major deliverable
3. Subdeliverable
4. Work package

Answer

Subsystems of a software development project constitute how the project will be organized and managed. It might be organized by phases or by the specific kinds of requirements identified in the scope statement.

Testing would be a major deliverable of a software development project. Another major deliverable might be System design and System installation.

The deliverable design tests typically divides into two subdeliverables: design manual tests and design automated tests.

Execute manual tests is a work package because it is an activity that can be easily assigned and estimated.

The breakdown for a WBS continues through multiple levels until the components can be estimated and resourced. Each level of deliverables includes the components that produce the next highest level in the tree.

As noted already, the lowest level of decomposition is the work package. It can be defined as a deliverable that can be measured, scheduled, budgeted, and has an accountable party assigned to it.

This is the level where the actual work can be assigned.

The WBS will be used as an input to numerous other planning

processes. It's the basis for estimating activity duration, assigning resources to activities, estimating work effort, and cost. Because the WBS is a graphical representation, it can be a better vehicle for communicating the project scope than the charter or scope statement.

The WBS puts boundaries around the project. Any work not defined in the WBS is considered outside the scope of the project. So a WBS is a tool that can be used to keep customers, team members, and stakeholders focused on what's included in the project scope.

Like a blueprint used to create a building, the WBS is the document that will be used to complete your project goal successfully.

Question

You're responsible for managing a project for your company that will set up a new web interface for ordering its products. Sequence the actions you would take to develop a WBS for this project.

Options:

A.   Assign the project the name Web Interface for Orders

B.   Divide the project into the phases database creation, application creation, web interface creation, and implementation and troubleshooting

C.   Identify design as one of the main deliverables for web interface creation phase

D.   Divide design into overall design, prototype, and detail design

E.   Decompose overall design component into the work required to complete it

Answer

Correct answer(s):

Assign the project the name Web Interface for Orders is ranked - This is the top level, encompassing the project as a whole. It embraces all the components into which the project is subdivided.

Divide the project into the phases database creation, applica-

tion creation, web interface creation, and implementation and troubleshooting is ranked - Subprojects may be the phases of the project life cycle or the different categories of requirements that are set for the project.

Identify design as one of the main deliverables for web interface creation phase is ranked - Deliverables are products that must be delivered to complete the project. Each of the subprojects or project subsystems will have key deliverables associated with it, which are identified as the third step in the process.

Divide design into overall design, prototype, and detail design is ranked - Deliverables are divided into subdeliverables. These are the tasks required to complete this deliverable, and noting them is the fourth step in the process.

Decompose overall design component into the work required to complete it is ranked - A work package can be defined as a deliverable that can be measured, scheduled, budgeted, and has an accountable party assigned to it.

3. Guidelines for WBS

As an IT project manager, you'll be under pressure. Once you start breaking your deliverables down into activities, it's tempting to immediately estimate how long they'll take so you can get people to work. But resist the temptation to rush through the process of creating a WBS. Otherwise, you may forget key deliverables or sequence tasks incorrectly because you haven't defined them adequately. There isn't one "right" way to complete a good WBS, but there are guidelines that can help.

First, don't try to complete the WBS by yourself to save time. A WBS created by a lone project manager frequently misses key components of the project. After all, you're probably not an expert on all the deliverables.

Also, you should involve team members because it's hard to get people to commit themselves to something they've had no input on.

And here's a practical tip: hold your WBS session in an area where there's plenty of space, rather than having people stand around a computer screen. Make sure you have a whiteboard, plenty of markers, sticky notes, and control of the meeting.

Second, work though all items at the second level before going down to lower levels. The entire work of the project should be represented at the high level. Then list all activities and keep breaking them down until you get to a level where the team feels comfortable that resources can be assigned and estimates can be completed. Sequencing, assigning resources, and estimating come later. WBS is simply about identifying the tasks at an assignable level.

To begin subdividing the project, you could ask whether there are logical ways in which the project could be carved up. A fairly typical approach would be to split the project into a number of phases or subprojects. For example, a software development project would typically have at least three major phases: design, testing, and marketing.

Asking certain questions can help identify such phases if they're not obvious. For example, is the budget for the project allocated in segments?

Are there identifiable milestones that could represent phases?

Question

What are some valid reasons for adopting a team approach to creating a WBS?

Options:

1. It's easier to get people to sign up for what they've been involved in creating
2. Trying to create a WBS on your own can result in some key deliverables being forgotten
3. It's quicker to work with others than on your own
4. You can get straight to assigning tasks

Answer

Option 1: *This is a correct option. The implementation of a project requires the commitment of the project team members. Getting this commitment will be easier if they were involved in planning the work.*

Option 2: This is a correct option. A project manager will not generally be an expert in all the deliverables, which makes it more likely that some deliverables will be forgotten.

Option 3: This option is incorrect. One reason why it's tempting for a project manager to develop a WBS alone is to save time. Unfortunately, rushing the WBS often leads to significant problems.

Option 4: This option is incorrect. High-level analysis of the project must come first. A danger to be avoided is that meetings rush too quickly to sequencing and assigning specific tasks.

An additional guideline is to remember that each item in a lower level is a component of the level above. Completion of all the items in the lower level should mean completion of the higher level. So, as a check, always review the items at the lower level and ask the team if completion of those items will complete the task at the next highest level. If it wouldn't, you haven't identified all of the lower level tasks.

Something you should beware of is getting too granular. You can't realistically micromanage a project down to the last detail. It's often the case that when a task can be expressed as a verb – for example, build, write, or document – then it can be considered a work package and need not be decomposed further.

The point is just to get to a level where activities can be easily assigned and estimated, and produce a meaningful deliverable.

A final principle to bear in mind is that not all major deliverables are subdividable to the same degree. For instance, a subdeliverable of managing communications is to resolve communication problems. That doesn't need to be broken down further – it's an activity that can be readily assigned.

But another deliverable of managing communications is to distribute information. This can be broken up into such work packages as documenting project procedures and attending relevant meetings. The point is that different deliverables require different levels of decomposition.

Question

Which are appropriate guidelines for creating an effective WBS?
Options:

1. Not every major deliverable is decomposed to the same level
2. You shouldn't decompose activities any further than to a level where they can be easily assigned and estimated, and produce a meaningful deliverable
3. When the element can be introduced by a verb, then it's probably a work package and doesn't need to be decomposed to a lower level
4. Each item in a lower level is a component of the level above
5. Start from the detailed tasks and work up to a more general level
6. Be as detailed as possible

Answer

Option 1: This is a correct option. This guideline means that it's a mistake to try to make a WBS too neat. Decomposing to the level of work packages may require more stages for some major deliverables than others.

Option 2: This is a correct option. This guideline counsels the project manager to avoid trying to manage every last detail. Once you get to the work package level, there's no need to go any further.

Option 3: This is a correct option. It's often the case that work packages can be stated by imperative verbs, such as develop, build, write, or document.

Option 4: This is a correct option. This rule implies that completion of all the items at the lower level should mean completion of the higher level.

Option 5: This option is incorrect. You start with the highest levels, making sure you've identified all the major phases or subprojects before you start subdividing down to detailed tasks.

Option 6: This option is incorrect. A danger to be avoided is getting too granular. If you get too detailed, you are mistakenly trying to micromanage the project.

4. The benefits of an effective WBS

The WBS is a valuable tool in many ways. It is essential because it creates a baseline to measure performance; that is to say, it sets milestones for progress. WBS also helps you determine the sequence in which work must be completed in order to finish the project as early as possible. WBS also clarifies who's responsible for what, and when.

In addition, the WBS can and should be an excellent tool for team building and communication. Team members can see the project's big picture and how their portion fits in. The direct link between a particular activity and a major project deliverable can also make clear the importance of the work of individual team members. As new team members are added to the project, the WBS can be used to bring them up to speed.

Equally important, the WBS provides an excellent tool for communicating with clients and stakeholders. People don't always comprehend the magnitude of a project until they see the diagram of the project objectives and the activities required to reach those objectives.

It's also an excellent tool to use when discussing staffing requirements or costs. It clearly shows what work is included in the project. If something isn't covered in the project objectives and supporting activities, it isn't part of the project.

Another benefit of a good WBS is that it can be turned into a template for future projects. Software development projects frequently have a similar life cycle, and what was done on a previous project can be used as a starting point for a new project.

Finally, as well as preventing critical work from being overlooked, an effective WBS also helps control change.

If the project team has a clear picture of the project objectives and the map to reach these objectives, they're less likely to go down a path unrelated to the project scope.

That's not to say that a WBS will prevent change. There are always changes during a project's life cycle. But a WBS will make it clear when a request is a change and not part of the original project scope.

Question

What are the benefits of an effective WBS?

Options:

1. It's an excellent tool for team building and communication
2. It's an excellent device for communicating with stakeholders and clients
3. It can serve as a template for future projects
4. It helps control change
5. It provides costing estimates
6. It works out the time each task will take

Answer

Option 1: *This is a correct option. The layout of the WBS enables team members to see how their activities fit into the overall project and how each individual contributes to the whole.*

Option 2: *This is a correct option. For example, sometimes stakeholders only grasp the full magnitude of a project when they see the work to be done laid out graphically in a good WBS.*

Option 3: *This is a correct option. Software development projects, for example, often have similar life cycles. So a well-developed WBS for one project may serve as a good basis for developing another.*

Option 4: *This is a correct option. An effective WBS controls change by clarifying what is part of the original scope of the project and what isn't.*

Option 5: *This option is incorrect. The WBS serves as a basis for such estimates. In itself, however, it only lays out the work to be done, without considering the cost involved in completing it.*

Option 6: *This option is incorrect. The WBS lays out the work to be done. It does not consider the time required to complete the work.*

5. Summary

Project planning starts by clarifying the project's scope with the help of the project charter that emerged from the initiation process. The scope planning process yields three deliverables: a scope statement, a scope management plan, and a work breakdown structure, or WBS.

The WBS subdivides the project into manageable and achievable components. It documents all the work that is required to successfully complete your project. A standard way of representing the WBS is by an organizational chart. On the top level is the project title. Below this come the subprojects. The next level down identifies major deliverables for each subproject. These are then divided into subdeliverables at the next level. The lowest level lists work packages, or specific tasks that can be meaningfully costed, estimated, and assigned.

Some of the benefits of creating a good WBS are that it enhances teamwork, improves communication with stakeholders, supplies a template for future projects, and helps control change.

Job Aid

Steps for Developing a Work Breakdown Structure

Purpose: *Use this job aid to review the steps for developing a WBS.*

Table 1: Steps involved in initiating a project	
Step	**Action to take**
Step 1	Give the project a name
Step 2	Identify the major phases or subprojects involved as the second level
Step 3	Indicate the major deliverables under each phase or subproject as the third level
Step 4	Keep subdividing these until you reach the level of work packages
Step 5	Assign numeric indicators to each level

SCHEDULE PLANNING FOR AN IT PROJECT

1. Sequencing activities

Once you have a work breakdown structure, or WBS, you are ready to begin developing a project schedule. This can be viewed as a three-step process. First, sequence your list of activities; second, estimate the durations of the activities; and third, develop your schedule using the critical path method. Sequencing the activities happens after the WBS because the assignable activities – work packages – have to be identified before you can put them in order.

The sequencing stage itself comprises three elements: **ordering** the list of activities, figuring out **dependencies** among them, and considering **constraints**.

Ordering activities means determining when tasks should be started, worked on, or completed. Most project tasks have some sort of logical sequence.

Once you've put tasks in a logical sequence, have the team check the sequence for anything that may stand out. For instance, someone might note that task 4 logically follows task 2, but it would be more desirable if it followed task 5 instead.

Or someone might identify a logical sequence that is impractical. Yes, it would be great to do task 11 and 14 at the same time, but if they require the same resource, that's not going to be possible. So, what's logical, what's desirable, and what's feasible are all relevant.

Once you have discerned the most logical, desirable, feasible sequence, you should consider if there are any project **constraints**.

For example, a constraint could be that your IT employees are in the middle of a mission-critical project. Key members of the IT team won't be available for additional project work for some time to come.

Or, the project involves rewiring part of your building, but a stakeholder mentions that the company is hosting several key clients for a week at some point during the project. This is another example of a high-level constraint. Constraints such as these could have a huge impact on the project's timeline and cost.

The third element in the sequencing process is more complex. You need to figure out **dependency relationships** between the activities. Perhaps one task cannot start until another is complete. For instance, the wiring needs to be laid before the servers can be installed. That would be an example of the most common kind of task dependency relationship: a finish-to-start relationship. But there are three other types of dependencies between predecessor and successor tasks: finish-to-finish, start-to-start, and start-to-finish.

Finish-to-start

In a finish-to-start relationship, the successor task cannot begin until the predecessor task has completed. This is the most common task relationship. It is the default setting on most project tracking software packages. For example, the user interface must be coded before the printing module can be developed.

Finish-to-finish

In a finish-to-finish relationship, the completion of the successor task depends on the completion of the predecessor. For example, a new product cannot be released to market until the customer manual is complete.

Start-to-start

In a start-to-start relationship, the start of the successor task depends on the start of the predecessor. The tasks can be worked in parallel, but if the first task is delayed, the successor task cannot start. For example, user guide documentation can only start when requirements definition starts.

Start-to-finish

In a start-to-finish relationship, the finish of the successor task is contingent on the start of its predecessor. This relationship is rarely used. Perhaps an example would be that a technical support task cannot be completed until the formation of the technical support team has started.

A careful examination of dependency relationships can shorten the schedule, particularly if two or more tasks can be done simultaneously rather than sequentially. However, doing this may add substantial risk to the project, which is the trade-off against potential schedule improvement.

For example, suppose you have planned a technology survey before designing a critical subsystem. But you then decide to begin the design and survey at the same time. You plan to use the survey results to validate your understanding of the state of the available technology.

If your knowledge of the available technology is current, this approach might work. But if the survey comes back indicating that your choice of system components is obsolete, you've actually jeopardized the schedule rather than improving it.

Clearly it's not enough to figure out the dependency relationships between tasks. They must be communicated to the team. So it's important that you create a pictorial representation of the tasks that shows all the dependencies.

Sequencing is best illustrated by means of a network diagram. Because you can actually see how the work flows, a network diagram is a great tool to develop with the project team.

A common method is to begin with a precedence table. This identifies all the WBS activities in order and indicates which depend on which. For example, suppose a project involves deploying 200 software applications at two locations and delivering user training. The delivery of training depends on identifying subject matter experts, interviewing them, identifying user requirements, and developing a training plan.

Then use the table to create a network diagram, either by hand or using project management software. Boxes represent the project activities, and arrows connect the boxes to depict the dependencies.

Determining task interdependencies is a team effort because each task leader will better understand what she needs as output from other tasks before she can finish her own effort. Task interdependencies drive the schedule because some tasks simply cannot begin until other tasks are completed.

In the previous example of deploying 200 software applications at two locations, the development of training content must be completed before the delivery of the training can begin. On the other hand, some tasks have no dependencies and can be accomplished in parallel with other tasks.

Question

Match type of dependency relationship with its description.

Options:

    A.   Start-to-finish

    B.   Start-to-start

    C.   Finish-to-start

    D.   Finish-to-finish

Targets:

    1. Task 1 must start so that task 2 can finish

    2. Task 2 can only start after task 1 starts

    3. Task 2 can only begin when task 1 has been completed

    4. Task 2 can only be completed after task 1 is completed

Answer

The start-to-finish dependency relationship is rare except in construction or manufacturing. In this type of dependency, the finish of the successor task is dependent on the start of its predecessor.

An example of a start-to-start dependency is requirements definition and user guide documentation. These tasks can run together, but if requirements definition is held up, so too is the user documentation task.

In a finish-to-start relationship, task 1 must be completed before task 2 can begin. For example, the training materials must be developed before the training can be delivered.

An example of a finish-to-finish relationship is how the release of a new product is contingent on the completion of the customer manual.

2. Estimating durations

Identifying all the dependencies between tasks and developing a network diagram to depict the flow of the project work is only the first step to creating your schedule. The second step, estimating activity durations, is vital to managing your project. The most common measurements used to define duration are days or weeks.

Before turning to the techniques you can use to complete your duration estimates, make sure that your team is clear about what activity duration means.

Activity duration is the total elapsed time to complete an activity. Consider a task that's estimated to take five days, based on an eight-hour day fully dedicated to that task. Notice that the actual duration estimate would be ten days if the resource assigned to the task is only spending four hours a day on the task.

You also need to be aware of the difference between workdays and calendar days. If your work week is Monday through Friday, and you have a four-day task starting on Friday, the duration for that task will be six calendar days, because no work will be done on Saturday and Sunday.

There is no one right way to do task duration estimates. Bear in mind that what's required is an estimate, not a 100% guarantee of the length of time each task will take to complete. There are three commonly used techniques for activity duration estimates: top down estimating, expert judgment, and quantitatively based estimating. Most projects use some combination of these estimating techniques depending on the kinds of project tasks involved.

Top down estimating

Top down estimating uses actual durations from similar activities on a previous project. This is applicable mainly at the early stages of project planning when you have limited information about the project.

It tends to be the least accurate means of obtaining an estimate because no two projects are exactly the same, and there's the risk that the project used to obtain the analogous estimates is not as similar as it seems.

Expert judgment

The expert judgment method is to use the people most familiar with the work to create the estimate. Ideally, the estimate is made by the team member who undertakes the task. If all team members haven't yet been identified, recruit people with expertise for the tasks you need estimated.

Quantitatively based estimating

Quantitatively based estimates use productivity rates to work out duration. If a typical cable crew can lay 3 miles of cable in a day, it should take 10 days to lay 30 miles of cable. This estimating technique can be very accurate for tasks that are repetitive and have a lot of productivity data.

Now the activity duration estimates can be included in the precedence table. And likewise, they can be added to the network diagram. Having created your network diagram with task durations, you are in a good position to move to the final stage of the scheduling process – schedule development.

Question

Match techniques for estimating duration to their descriptions.

Options:

   A.   Top down
   B.   Expert judgment
   C.   Quantitatively based

Targets:

   1. Use actual durations from similar activities on a previous project
   2. Use the people most familiar with the work to create

the estimate
3. Use productivity rate to work out duration

Answer

Top down estimating assumes duration can be predicted based on previous projects. The drawback is that no two projects are exactly alike.

Expert judgment can be a good method because those who are assigned a tasks are usually best placed to know how long it will take.

A quantitatively based method requires information on the productivity rate and formulas to gauge duration.

3. Developing the schedule

Having sequenced the activities and estimated their durations, your final schedule planning step is to develop the schedule. You establish a start date and a finish date for every activity. Given the other schedule planning processes you've completed, this might not seem like much of a challenge. But, in fact, putting together all the data and creating a project schedule is a complex process. Fortunately, there are techniques available to help. The most important one is the critical path method.

The **critical path method**, or CPM, is a mathematically based technique for calculating the earliest possible finish date for a project. It works by identifying the longest activity sequence path in the project. That will be the path that determines the project's finish date. As project manager, this is the path you want to monitor most.

Recall the earlier example of a project to deploy software applications to 200 systems at two locations and train users. As you'll remember from the precedence table, training can only be delivered when the software has been deployed at both locations. Assuming deployment and delivery of training take a day each, it seems the project might take just two days.

However, delivery of training depends on another sequence. The training content must have been developed, which presupposes the identification of user training requirements. And that requires interviewing subject matter experts, which assumes they have been identified. If developing content takes two days and the rest one day each, the project takes six days.

CPM helps you figure out project duration. Taking data from the precedence table, you create a network diagram. Nodes represent start and finish of activities, and arrows give durations. In the previous example, one path is just to deploy the software and deliver the training – taking only two days. But this ignores tasks on which delivery of training depends. The longest path is the critical path, and this shows that the overall duration of the project is six days.

In addition to calculating the overall time to complete the project and identifying tasks on the critical path, CPM supplies other useful data. You can determine which tasks can start late or can take longer than planned without impacting the project end date.

A problem for CPM arises when the total project duration is longer than your target project completion date.

Duration compression scheduling techniques help reduce completion time without reducing project scope. One such technique is fast tracking, where more things are done at the same time in order to finish a job earlier than planned. Sequential relationships are replaced by parallel ones.

Project management software can be used to help you schedule projects and finish them on time.

Some benefits of using project management software are automation of tasks and calculations and the availability of schedule templates. The software also facilitates the electronic distribution of information over a network or intranet to stakeholders, team members, and clients.

Question

Sequence the steps in creating a project schedule.

Options:

    A.   Put activities in order

    B.   Consider constraints

    C.   Figure out dependencies

D.   Use top down estimating technique or other technique for determining durations of activities

E.   Use the critical path method and project management software to develop schedule

Answer

Put activities in order is ranked - The order in which tasks should be started, worked on, or completed is the starting point for scheduling.

Consider constraints is ranked - Once you've identified the most logical, desirable, feasible sequence, you should consider any relevant project constraints, such as whether the same resources needed for different tasks.

Figure out dependencies is ranked - There are four possible dependency relationships between activities. The most common is finish-to-start, where one task cannot begin until another is completed.

Use top down estimating technique or other technique for determining durations of activities is ranked - The top down method is one technique for estimating activity durations. It relies on the actual durations from similar activities on a previous project.

Use the critical path method and project management software to develop schedule is ranked - Using the critical path method would be the last step in creating a project. It uses the longest path through a project to calculate the earliest possible finish date. Project management software can help you create your schedule.

4. Summary

There are three steps to developing a project schedule. First, sequence your list of activities, consider project constraints, and work out the dependencies between the activities. This involves creating a precedence table and network diagram. Second, estimate the durations of the activities using top down estimating, expert judgment, or quantitatively based estimation. The durations can now be added to the precedence table and network diagram.

Third, develop your schedule using the critical path method. This involves working out the longest path through the plan and using this as a guide to overall project duration. Duration compression may be useful where the critical path suggests a duration beyond the required target date. Project management software may be used at any stage of planning the project schedule.

Job Aid
The Three Steps to Creating a Project Schedule
Purpose: *Use this aid to review the steps involved in creating a project schedule.*

Table 1: Three steps to creating a project schedule		
Step number	**Step**	**Associated actions**
1	Sequence activities	Put activities in order, consider constraints, and figure out dependencies among activities.
2	Estimate durations	Determine which technique to use for estimating activity durations. For example, use top down estimating, expert judgment, quantitatively based estimating, or a combination of these.
3	Develop schedule	Choose the appropriate technique to develop the project schedule. Critical path method is the most commonly used. Or, if you need to bring forward the project finish date, duration compression can be used. Project management software is useful for all stages of schedule planning and development.

COST PLANNING FOR AN IT PROJECT

1. Resources planning

Suppose you're the manager of a new IT project. You've worked out the project scope, the tasks involved, and the schedule, but what about costs? Project managers not only have to manage the scope and duration of the project, they also have to manage the costs. If you develop a plan to identify and manage your costs, it will help you complete your project within the approved budget. In an ideal world, there would be no limit to funds, and projects would never be short of money. But in the real world, projects are constrained by budgets, and cost overruns have to be avoided. There's never enough money, and, as a project manager, you're always expected to do more with less. It can be very difficult to go back and ask for more money once a project is underway. So it's vital to do the best job possible when planning for the funds you'll need.

But before you can begin cost planning, you need to determine your resource requirements – what labor, equipment, and materials are needed. For example, how many person-hours and how many additional PCs will the project need?

Fortunately, you should be able to use inputs from previous planning processes to help identify your resource needs. For example, you might know from the requirement-gathering stage that the system you'll be creating has to be browser-based. So you immediately know that you'll need human resources to recruit web programmers.

You may also be able to draw on resource information from similar projects in the past. That will point you in the right direction. It's a good idea to identify the resource requirements for your project under the three categories – labor, equipment, and materials. You can place these requirements beside each work package in the work breakdown structure, or WBS. The table representing this information is called a Resource Assignment Matrix. For example, consider such a document for a software development project. For each of the various tasks, it should tell you how many programmers are required, how many testers, how many technical writers, and what equipment.

Question

Which actions can help you determine the resource requirements for your project?

Options:

1. Use inputs from previous planning processes
2. Consult resources from similar projects in the past
3. Estimate costs of each of the project's work packages
4. Create a Resource Assignment Matrix
5. Create the project schedule

Answer

Option 1: *This is a correct option. Using inputs from previous planning processes entails gleaning information from the findings of the requirements-gathering stage of the project initiation phase.*

Option 2: *This is a correct option. Resources needed for previous, similar projects can serve as a guide for a new project.*

Option 3: *This is not a correct option. You need to know the resource requirements before you can estimate the costs.*

Option 4: *This is a correct option. The Resource Assignment Matrix helps you determine at a glance the labor, equipment, and materials needed for each work package in the WBS.*

Option 5: *This is not a correct option. Schedule requirements might sometimes have resource implications, but developing the schedule is not designed to help you determine the resource requirements for the project.*

2. Cost estimating techniques

Now you've documented your project resource requirements, you can start estimating cost. This is the process of determining how much money you'll spend on the resources needed to complete the project. But remember that cost estimates are just approximations – not exact predictions. Still, you can increase the accuracy of your estimates by using all the data and tools available to you. Three methods of estimating cost that you may use are top-down estimating, bottom-up estimating, and parametric modeling.

Top-down estimating gets its name from the fact that it estimates the cost of the project at a high level, rather than by working out the cost of individual work packages. This kind of estimate is typically done as part of a business case in the initiation process, or during the early planning stage of scope planning, when not many details on the project are available.

The method involves comparing the proposed project to a similar project from the past. For example, perhaps a new desktop tool project is compared to a previous desktop tool project. The costs should be similar once some adjustment for inflation is made.

Top-down estimates tend to have a very low level of accuracy. This is largely because projects are rarely as similar as they might seem. But the method is still valuable because it's based on experience, rather than guesswork. The important thing is to make sure everyone realizes how imprecise the estimate is.

So-called bottom-up estimating is the most definitive technique. It works by estimating the cost of each work package in the WBS and adding these costs together to get the total project cost.

Cost estimates are based on work effort, which is the total time it would take for a person to complete the task if they did nothing else from the time they started until the task was complete. A work effort estimate is also referred to as a person-hour estimate.

You can create a Project Work Effort Matrix to represent the relevant information. Notice that the relation between activity duration and work effort is not completely straightforward.

For example, the work effort for writing a technical document might be 20 hours, but if the technical writer can only allocate two hours a day to the task, then the activity duration will be ten days. A disadvantage of bottom-up estimating is that the method is time-consuming, and sufficient information will not be available early in the project.

A third technique for estimating cost is parametric modeling. Parametric modeling uses a mathematical model based on known parameters to predict the cost of a project. This method has the advantage that the models tend to be fast, easy to use, and objective.

Parametric modeling generally uses such parameters as industry standards related to cost per unit installed, cost per machine delivered, and so on. But this approach doesn't always work for IT projects because of the variables within the technology.

For example, in the case of an IT project, a parameter might be cost per unit of code. But lines of code don't always reflect the productivity, the number of servers, or even the number of programmers assigned to an activity.

Accurately costing IT projects is certainly a challenge. That's because more or less everything connected with IT fluctuates, whether it's memory requirements, software versions, or processor speed.

Another challenge is the difficulty of measuring productivity in IT because of the wide variation in the types of work that an IT project may entail.

An additional challenge when it comes to IT costing is the built-in uncertainty of testing. Testing is undoubtedly necessary to ensure things work the way they should in the final product. But specific tests are difficult to justify because it's hard to predict exactly what problems the testing will capture.

Question

Match cost estimation techniques to their descriptions.

Options:

    A.   Top-down estimating

    B.   Bottom-up estimating

C.   Parametric estimating

Targets:
1. Compare the proposed project to a previous project that seems broadly similar
2. Estimate the cost of each work package and add these costs together to get the total project cost
3. Perform an overall estimate of the project using design parameters and mathematical algorithms

Answer

The top-down method offers a high level cost estimate based on past projects. It's useful because it can be done at an early stage of the project, but it can be very inaccurate because projects tend to be unique. This is the most detailed and definitive technique. It's more accurate than other methods, but also more time consuming.

This method often bases unit costs on industry standards. Its models are easy to use, objective, and repeatable, but the variables within IT can make it difficult to apply.

3. Summary

Cost planning entails developing a plan to identify and manage costs that will help you complete your project within the approved budget.

You should begin by clarifying your project resource requirements – labor, equipment, and materials. Once you've determined the requirements for completing the project, you're ready to start estimating cost.

Three methods of estimating cost may be used: top-down estimating, bottom-up estimating, and parametric modeling. The top-down method relies on what similar projects have cost in the past; the bottom-up method adds up the costs of all the individual work packages; and parametric modeling uses industry standards to cost project parameters.

IT PROJECT MANAGEMENT ESSENTIALS: EXECUTING IT PROJECTS

Have you ever known of a project plan that seemed fine on paper but didn't fulfill its objectives? Such a plan may not have been properly executed. The execution phase of an IT project is when the work gets underway and project managers must transform plans into actions. To satisfy the objectives laid out in the project plan, IT managers must develop high performing teams, keep work on track, ensure vital information flows as it should, and monitor quality.

As a project manager, you must guide projects to successful completion. This involves developing your project team, communicating effectively, and monitoring performance to make sure your results come as close to your plan objectives as possible. Building a strong project team goes a long way toward making this happen. Planning both your communications and your quality control measures are also crucial to success.

In this course, you'll learn about strategies for developing and maintaining a cohesive project team. A cohesive team is one in which members work well together and therefore achieve high performance levels. The strategies managers use to explain project purpose, monitor performance, and deal with problems all affect cohesion.

You'll also learn about the different ways project managers can improve execution through their communications. Project performance depends greatly on the flow of information. Managers must communicate effectively in a number of directions to ensure all stakeholders get the data they need.

The issue of quality on IT projects is also addressed in this course. Ensuring the quality of deliverables takes advance preparation and planning. You'll learn how a written communications plan detailing objectives, responsibilities, procedures, and metrics will keep projects on track and meeting quality goals.

Executing an IT Project

1. Maintaining a Cohesive IT Project Team
2. Communicating during IT Project Execution
3. Keeping Quality on Track during IT Project Execution

MAINTAINING A COHESIVE IT PROJECT TEAM

1. The execution phase

The execution phase of an IT project is when the work gets going and plans are transformed into actions. When it's time for this phase to begin, a project manager with highly experienced team members, each with expertise in particular knowledge areas, may be tempted to just let the team loose to do what they do best. But, in general, a totally hands-off approach is unlikely to result in a team that delivers high-quality results under tight budgets and schedules.

To get results during the execution phase, IT managers must work hard, plan ahead, and employ effective strategies to build and maintain cohesive project teams.

In the course of performing their duties, IT project managers may need to consider and interact with other functions to execute a project plan.

The project manager's overall duty is to drive the project plan to successful completion. To do this, project managers have specific responsibilities during execution:

- manage the various processes involved in the project
- make sure milestones are met on time and within budget
- continually verify that the project remains in scope and on target
- monitor the quality of deliverables to ensure they meet

company standards and will satisfy the end user

- track resource use against the project plan to ensure sufficient resources will be available until the end of the project
- build a cohesive team by helping team members understand interdependencies, manage conflict productively, and work well together, and
- facilitate communication with other project stakeholders, including other departments, customers, and executive management

In large companies, communication and negotiation between departments is typical. For example, for a given IT project, business development may be involved in purchasing hardware, software, or services. The quality assurance department may set up testing procedures, the documentation department may coordinate information related to user manuals, and HR may be tasked with monitoring and adjusting human resources as needed. In smaller companies, it may be the project manager who is responsible for some or all of these responsibilities.

2. Explaining project purpose

Often, the biggest challenge project managers face is to get everyone on their IT project teams to work together toward a common goal. As a project manager, you need to start the execution phase by focusing on **building and managing a cohesive team**. Three key strategies can help: explain the project purpose, monitor performance, and act on problems.

Explain the project purpose

Typically, project managers explain the purpose of the project at a project kickoff meeting. The kickoff should answer the key concerns everyone has about the project: who you are, how the work will be accomplished, and what you expect for results. The kickoff meeting provides the opportunity to begin forming a cohesive team.

Monitor performance

The way in which you monitor performance can affect team

cohesion. IT teams are often composed of competent, strong-willed individuals. It's important that your monitoring procedures demonstrate your trust in them while ensuring projects remain on track.

Act on problems

To be cohesive, your team members need to work well with each other, and they need to be able to rely on you, as their manager. They need to feel confident that you're capable and will resolve any conflicts or other problems without delay.

A well-planned kickoff meeting is a project manager's best chance to set the right tone, get team members comfortable with each other, and convey the same overall message to everyone involved. The kickoff can be instrumental in **explaining the project purpose** to participants in a way that provides them with a firm foundation from which to work.

Many of the project stakeholders – such as the executive sponsors, vendors, customers, or other guests – may be included in the kickoff. In some cases, the kickoff meeting may be the last time all stakeholders meet to discuss the project.

Kickoff meeting structure

A good kickoff meeting can go a long way towards building a cohesive team. It's likely that any successful project kickoff meeting will begin with introductions, go on to explore what is expected of the project, and end with the project manager answering questions. The kickoff is often a key part of the forming stage of team development, where team members get oriented to the project's objectives, the project manager, and each other.

Kickoff meetings can be structured in a number of ways. A typical recommended sequence contains six main elements:

- Begin the meeting by welcoming the team members and letting them know you look forward to working together. Then set the stage for the meeting – explain what will be covered and how.
- Introduce yourself and get everyone else to do the

same. Typically, introductions should include role on the team, areas of expertise, and some brief background. Your own introduction may help give the others a sense of the amount of detail to provide.

- Invite sponsors, clients, executives, and any other stakeholders who are guests to say a few words to the team. In many cases, having guests speak early will be necessary because some may not be able to stay for the whole meeting.
- Provide a project overview by discussing the project scope, summarizing the key deliverables, and touching on the schedule and budget at a high level. This ensures all team members get the same initial big picture view of the project.
- Communicate your expectations as manager regarding how the team will function. Don't go into great detail – just let everyone know how you work and what you expect from them in terms of meetings, progress reports, and providing input.
- Give team members a chance to ask questions of you and of any guests such as sponsors, clients, or executive stakeholders. Leaving questions until the end is fine, but be cautious, as it's also the surest way to run out of time for them.

Olaf is an IT project manager conducting his first kickoff meeting. He begins by telling everyone his name and that he's leading this project.

He welcomes the team, expresses confidence in them, and asks them to introduce themselves by stating their names, where they're from, and what areas they have expertise in.

After the introductions, Olaf introduces the executive sponsor for the project, who gives the team background information as to how the project initiative was conceived.

Olaf did fairly well by getting everyone to introduce themselves and going to the guest speaker early on. But he failed to fully introduce himself at the beginning. He should have provided some brief background for those team members who didn't already know him. He also could have done a better job of setting the stage for the meeting – letting people know what to expect before going on to the introductions.

Question

Which examples illustrate how kickoff meetings can be effectively conducted to explain the project purpose?

Options:

1. Convey a high-level overview of the project scope and your expectations to everyone at the same time
2. Welcome the participants, introduce team members to each other, set the stage for the meeting, and allow guest speakers to address the team
3. Allow time for questions and answers
4. Go into detail about the expectations you have for each team member
5. Send out a kickoff presentation instead of having a real-time meeting

Answer

Option 1: This is a correct option. The project overview – including scope, key deliverables, schedule, and budget – should be communicated at a high level.

Option 2: This is a correct option. You should begin the meeting by welcoming the team and introducing yourself and others.

Option 3: This is a correct option. To effectively explain the project purpose, you need to allow participants to get clarification by asking questions.

Option 4: This is an incorrect option. You don't need to go into great detail about individual expectations. Just let everyone know how you work and what you expect from them in terms of meetings, progress reports, and providing input.

Option 5: This is an incorrect option. While a presentation is often helpful, it should only be part of a kickoff meeting. The team still needs to meet each other and be able to ask questions.

3. Monitoring performance

Monitoring performance is key to managing any work activity. When working with a project team, it's particularly important to monitor performance in ways that build cohesion, rather than breaking it down. From the team members' perspective, monitoring performance is one of the most visible tasks a project manager performs. If project managers seem to be hovering, managing every little detail, reserving all decision-making power for themselves, and distrusting of team members' actions, cohesion will be lost.

There are several techniques you can use to maintain team cohesion when monitoring performance:

- set clear performance expectations so everyone understands what, how, and when things must be done
- get progress reports from your team members
- check and validate progress on deliverables, and
- reward superior performance fairly and consistently

When monitoring performance, you must give support, apply standards, and take corrective action fairly and consistently. One key to being fair is being clear about **performance expectations**. You can't expect your team members to hit targets if they don't know exactly what the targets are.

Make sure everyone understands what needs to be done, how it needs to be done, and when it must be completed by, so that neither you nor they are disappointed when milestones roll around. At the kickoff meeting, you explain how team members are expected to report progress. You may have a specific progress report template, or you may want your team to report their progress at weekly meetings. But you may need specific data to be provided so that you can include it in your own project progress reports. Whatever you decide, make sure your team members are clear about how they should report to you.

How you check and validate the team's progress is important. If you do it poorly, you'll seem to be hovering and getting in the way of work. In the case of IT professionals, you often need to step back and let people do the work they were assigned without micromanaging. Often, the result is what matters rather than the particular method used to achieve it. Managing things too closely may just slow progress and project a lack of trust.

Question

Consider this example. Martin, an IT project manager, requires his employees to complete a standardized progress report form every day. Many elements of the form are unchanged from week to week, but team members still have to compile the same metrics.

Do you think Martin is validating and checking progress in the best possible way?

Options:

1. Yes
2. No

Answer

While Martin has a clear process in place for getting progress reports, micromanaging the project team this way is a mistake. The team members have to compile the same data over and over, which is not the best use of their time.

As Martin may learn, when validating progress it may be enough to informally check in every couple of days to learn how things are going, offer any assistance needed, and clarify any requirements.

This light touch simultaneously demonstrates that you care about team members' work and that you trust them to accomplish it on their own. In general, if there's no impact on scope, schedule, budget, or quality, you should let people do things their own way.

As you monitor progress, keep employees on track by rewarding superior performance. Many possibilities for rewards programs exist, from gold stars to monetary bonuses. Whichever method you choose, apply it consistently to avoid favoritism. Give performance feedback – both good and bad – in a timely manner. Your team trusts you to be fair in rewards and feedback. Unfairly applied rewards lead to disgruntled employees, interpersonal conflict, and low morale.

Question

What can you do as IT project manager to maintain team cohesiveness when monitoring performance?

Options:

1. Ask team members for progress reports at weekly meetings and require them to bring hard data on resource usage
2. Establish at the kickoff that everyone must submit deliverables in a standard format by 4:00 p.m. on due dates
3. Check in informally on progress and allow team members to make most decisions on their own
4. Reward outstanding achievement publicly with both acknowledgment and a monetary bonus
5. Use your budget to encourage those team members you think will go on to be project managers
6. State early on that you must approve all decisions and that you'll be watching everyone closely

Answer

Option 1: This is a correct option. Verbal updates at weekly meetings may be sufficient. It's also reasonable for a project manager to require some hard data from team members, to pass along in his own progress reports.

Option 2: This is a correct option. Setting clear expectations removes uncertainty. Announcing them at the kickoff means everyone is given the same instructions.

Option 3: This is a correct option. Allowing people the maximum amount of leeway in doing their jobs shows confidence in them and promotes cohesion.

Option 4: This is a correct option. Rewarding superior performance in public motivates team members. Monetary bonuses are fine rewards, as long as a manager is consistent and fair in the criteria for giving them.

Option 5: This is an incorrect option. Rewards should be given for outstanding performance, not to encourage your favorite team members.

Option 6: *This is an incorrect option. If a project manager hovers over the team and micromanages the project, it demonstrates a lack of trust and will hurt team cohesion.*

4. Acting on problems

Inevitably, once a planned project comes into contact with the real world – in this case, your team – problems arise. Scheduling conflicts, interpersonal problems, and disagreements over technical approaches can all affect progress and team cohesion. If you pretend problems don't exist or if you avoid addressing issues until they reach crisis proportions, you'll lose credibility and your team will lose faith in your ability to manage. To maintain cohesion on any project team, you must **act on problems**.

Many types of problems can arise on an IT project team:

- personal disputes between team members
- differences of opinion about what's required, such as suitability of deliverables, what should be included and excluded, and which design approach is best
- unhappy or disgruntled team members
- competition and conflict over resources such as people, equipment, facilities, and budgets
- scheduling conflicts, such as when employees are committed to too many projects at the same time
- conflicting priorities, such as when the budget department is most concerned with keeping costs down while quality assurance is focused on fewer known issues, and
- inadequate performance from one or more team members

Project-related conflicts usually revolve around scope, schedule, and resources. For example, a scope conflict might occur if two team members disagree about the number of features a particular software program should include. Or, if the program targets multiple customers, conflicts may arise as to which features to focus on.

IT team members are often engaged in more than one project at a time, and meeting milestones for each project may cause scheduling conflicts.

Conflicts may also arise when resources, people, and equipment are shared with other departments. Different departments in the organization may have different priorities, particularly when matters of budget are involved.

For example, the quality department may want more time to be spent debugging a program before release, while the marketing department may want more resources to be applied to designing the look and feel of the product to ensure saleability.

Well-functioning teams deal with conflict openly and use it as an opportunity for learning and growth. A few key tips can help you deal with project team conflicts:

- understand the source of the conflict by getting all the facts so you know what's causing the issue
- define the problem simply and clearly
- establish what would be a solution for each of the involved parties, and
- work with all parties to achieve a consensus solution

Understand the source

Get the information you need to ensure you fully understand what's causing the conflict. Learn what's really behind the dispute or what the root cause of the problem is instead of making a snap judgment.

Define the problem

Work with everyone involved to define the problem and conflict simply and clearly before moving on to develop a solution.

Establish what would be a solution

Establish what a solution would look like for each of the involved parties. Try to be sure that your solution will truly solve the problem for everyone.

Achieve consensus

Achieve a consensus solution that everyone can agree to without reluctance. A collaborative approach usually yields longer lasting results.

It's easier and better for maintaining team progress to deal with problems as they arise, rather than allowing them to accumulate. For example, putting off conflicts related to budget and schedule may multiply the problem, as these sorts of issues naturally become more acute towards the end of a project as resources run out.

When you hear about an issue, act on it. Team members will be frustrated if they know you're aware of a problem and not dealing with it. If you want team members to trust and respect you, help them get their jobs done and resolve their problems.

What you cannot do is avoid dealing with conflict. This is also true when dealing with inadequate performance of team members.

Unlike rewarding superior performance – which should be done publicly for maximum effect – inadequate performance should be dealt with in private to avoid exacerbating problems by making the person angry and defensive.

Question

If you observe members of your IT project team arguing, how might you act on problems to build team cohesion?

Options:

1. Get the facts and describe what the problem is based on those facts
2. Help involved parties come to a consensus about how to deal with the issue
3. Consider the types of solutions to the problem that might work
4. Be patient and wait until the situation resolves itself
5. Wait until the problem impacts the schedule before taking action

Answer

Option 1: *This is a correct option. It's a good idea to try to understand the true source of a problem before attempting to deal with a conflict situation.*

Option 2: *This is a correct option. It's important to act on conflict* *quickly. Resolving a conflict by achieving consensus can result in better solutions because individuals are involved in the final decision.*

Option 3: *This is a correct option. Before you can come to a consensus about what to do, you need to have some options to bring to the table.*

Option 4: *This is an incorrect option. Problems rarely solve themselves and avoiding them will only make you look bad to your team.*

Option 5: *This is an incorrect option. You should take action as soon as possible and not wait for problems to escalate.*

5. Summary

A cohesive project team is one in which team members work well together and are therefore more productive. Throughout the lifetime of a project, there are actions managers can take to create and maintain a cohesive team: explaining the purpose of the project, monitoring performance, and acting on problems.

The kickoff meeting provides the best opportunity to explain project purpose in such a way that everyone gets the same big picture information. During monitoring, the emphasis should be on keeping progress on track without micromanaging. Finally, when acting on problems, it's important to remember that team cohesion is based on trust and your team members count on you to act quickly and fairly to resolve issues that arise.

Job Aid

Strategies for Building Cohesive IT Teams

Purpose: *Use this job aid to help you recall what actions to take when using the three strategies for building cohesive IT teams.*

Strategy 1: Explaining project purpose

Typically, project managers explain the purpose of the project at the project kickoff meeting. The kickoff should answer the key concerns everyone has about the project: who you are, how the work will be accomplished, and what you expect for results. The kickoff meeting provides the opportunity to begin forming a cohesive team.

A typical recommended sequence for a kickoff meeting contains six main elements:

- **Welcome** – Begin the meeting by welcoming the team and set the stage for the meeting.
- **Introductions** – Introduce yourself and get everyone else to do the same. Typically, introductions should include role on the team, areas of expertise, and some brief background.
- **Guest speakers** – Invite guests to say a few words early in the meeting, especially in cases where they may not be able to stay the entire time.
- **Project overview** – Discuss the project scope, key deliverables, schedule, and budget at a high level.
- **Project manager expectations** – Communicate your expectations regarding how the team will function, how you work, and what you expect from them in terms of meetings, progress reports, and providing input.
- **Question and answer** – Give team members a chance to ask questions of you and of any guests.

Strategy 2: Monitoring performance

The way in which you monitor performance can affect team cohesion. IT teams are often composed of competent, strong-willed individuals. It's important that your monitoring procedures demonstrate your trust in your team while ensuring projects remain on track.

- **Get progress reports from your team members** – In the case of IT project teams, you'll typically want progress reports at weekly meetings.
- **Set clear performance expectations** – Make sure everyone understands what needs to be done, how it needs to be done, and when it must be completed by.
- **Check and validate progress on deliverables** – Let people do the work they were assigned without micromanaging. A light touch demonstrates trust.
- **Reward superior performance** – Whichever reward method you choose, the important thing is to apply it

fairly and consistently. The same goes for addressing inadequate performance.

Strategy 3: Acting on problems

The third strategy is to act on problems. To build and maintain the trust of your project team members, you need to demonstrate your competence and integrity. You can't allow problems to go unchecked or pretend problems don't exist. If you do, your team will lose faith in your ability to manage.

Many types of problems can arise on an IT project team. Conflicts related to scope, schedule, and priorities are among the most common. Addressing and resolving conflict quickly builds cohesion because it demonstrates you care and you're competent.

Your approach to conflict will be more effective if you keep in mind four key tips:

- **Understand the source** – Get all the information you need to truly understand the problem and what's causing it.
- **Define the problem** – Work with the various parties to clearly and simply define the problem.
- **Establish a solution** – Develop a clear statement of what would be considered a solution by all parties.
- **Work to achieve consensus** – Try to get everyone involved to agree and accept the solution.

COMMUNICATING DURING IT PROJECT EXECUTION

1. Role of communication

IT projects can be complex, so effective communication is essential. How would you feel if you put a lot of effort and money into developing a well-organized database for your IT project, only to find out that another IT team had already compiled the same information? Such a situation emphasizes the importance of good communication, not only within an IT project team but also with those outside it.

Many different internal and external stakeholders need to know where things stand, what decisions have been made, and what issues arise. Over the life of a project, project managers must take in and communicate information **downward**, **sideways**, and **upward**.

Downward

Downward communication includes providing clear instruction and explaining the issues to the team, including listening and acting on feedback and promoting good relations among team members.

Project managers do this verbally at meetings and throughout daily contact. They also communicate in writing through project plans, agendas, meeting minutes, schedules, and e-mail updates.

Sideways

Project managers must communicate sideways with other project managers and with vendors and clients to secure project resources. These communications are likely to be formal and informal, written and verbal.

Some, such as negotiating with vendors and clients relative to contracts and statements of work, require a degree of diplomacy and the development of good relationships.

Upward

Project managers communicate upward to sponsors and executive management. They provide information on risks and issues encountered. They also report on project progress and its adherence to schedule and budget.

In addition to e-mail, the more formal approaches such as communication plans, written status reports, and face-to-face project reviews provide much of this information.

Some communications are written and some are verbal, and they can be formal or informal to varying degrees. Formal communications include progress reports, status reports, meeting minutes, project audits, presentations, and team meetings. Informal communications include memos, notes, e-mails, one-on-one meetings, casual conversations, and phone calls. Informal does not mean unimportant however. Memos, notes, and e-mails can have legally binding implications even though they are informal communications.

Communications are a key component of any project. During planning, project managers should create a communications plan that identifies all the project stakeholders, their information needs, and the format and timing of the communications.

The communications plan can be used to define communication procedures and guidelines. For example, guidelines might indicate whether e-mails are preferred over phone calls for certain types of information, or how long someone should wait for a response before escalating an issue.

The communications plan may also specify contingencies if the planned communication methods don't work. For instance, it could specify that for urgent situations individuals should be contacted at home by phone, and provide the means to contact them. It should also define what an urgent situation is.

A typical communications plan defines the project stakeholders, what each needs to know, and the way in which communications will be handled. The communications plan can be as simple as a table or a spreadsheet with column headings for the various stakeholders across the top and the type of information down the left side. In the cells of the table, you can put a brief description of what information will be provided, when it will be provided, and how.

Communications plans can take simpler forms as well. Whatever format is used, the important thing is to clearly convey how project communications will be handled.

Any additional notes that may help define communications procedures should be included with the plan even if they don't fit neatly into the table categories.

For example, you may need to specify communication guidelines for members of the team who are located in other countries. An additional note containing the various time zones that team members are in may be useful.

E-mail communication guidelines

You may use or have considered ideas such as labeling the e-mail subject line as "immediate action required" for urgent items. Of course, defining what constitutes "urgent" is important. You might also consider putting "FYI" in the subject line when e-mails are updates of information with no response needed.

2. Project team meetings

One of the primary goals of project communication is disseminating information about the project. It's important to ensure the right method is used to communicate, and that the right amount of information is provided to inform but not overwhelm recipients. There are three main ways project information is distributed: project team meetings, status reports, and project reviews.

Project team meetings are the standard vehicle for project managers to convey information downward in an organization. Managers use kickoff meetings to initiate projects and then often follow with weekly team meetings to keep projects on track and update information.

Project team meetings allow team members to voice concerns on a weekly basis.

Meetings provide a forum for discussing issues as they arise and are the best tool for maintaining ongoing communication.

They help build and maintain strong team relationships, which can be particularly important in long-term projects.

To be effective, team meetings should be planned and organized. Simply gathering once a week for a chat is not enough to keep a project on track.

Team meetings are a manager's best chance to provide direction, clarify questions, and facilitate team member interaction to improve the performance of a team. If they're well run, they can propel a project forward.

If instead they're disorganized, unfocused, poorly run, and inefficient, they can just as easily slow a project to a crawl.

Well-run project team meetings require careful planning, advance actions, and use of several best practices:

- Set a regular day and time for the team meeting so team members can schedule around it. Consider getting input from team members about what might be a good day for most people.
- Emphasize the importance of attendance. Make it clear that team members should attend or send someone else in their place.
- Prepare and distribute an agenda in advance. The agenda should specify who's attending, how the meeting will be run, what the goals are, what subjects will be covered, and how much time will be allotted to each topic.

- Start and end on time. If certain issues that arise are taking too long to resolve, this may mean setting them aside and addressing after the meeting or setting up a separate meeting to address them.
- Follow your agenda and use your facilitation skills to keep the meeting on track. IT team members are busy people, so meetings that waste their time will be a source of frustration.
- Encourage participation. Avoid letting a few team members monopolize the meeting and directly encourage quieter members to speak up.
- Summarize the meeting. Wrap things up with a verbal summary of what was discussed and accomplished, and then send out written meeting minutes afterward.

Question

What are the benefits for project managers of being able to conduct effective team meetings?

Options:

1. They can facilitate team member interaction and improve the performance of their teams
2. They can resolve issues and problems more effectively
3. They can reduce the number of meetings needed
4. They can improve communications between the team and its sponsors

Answer

Option 1: *This is a correct option. Well-run team meetings help improve performance by ensuring everyone is working with the same information and by giving team members the chance to build better working relationships.*

Option 2: *This is a correct option. Conducting regular team meetings allows project managers to find out about possible issues and problems and deal with these in a timely manner.*

Option 3: *This is an incorrect option. Fewer meetings is not a benefit. Team meetings build relationships, solve problems, and keep everyone on the team up to date.*

Option 4: *This is an incorrect option. Conducting effective team*

110

meetings won't necessarily improve communications with parties outside of the team.

Often with IT projects, you have a core group of people working together on a daily basis while other team members are spread around the country or world. Project managers whose teams are virtual, or have virtual members, face unique challenges in project team meetings. For virtual team participants to collaborate effectively, share information, and develop and maintain good team relationships, it's even more vital to plan and facilitate meetings well and employ the right communications technology.

Virtual team members may come from different regions, countries, and cultures and they may never meet each other in person. Even without language and cultural hurdles, virtual team participants typically must forego many important nonverbal cues such as body language and facial expressions. For people to work well together in this situation, they must depend on technology to bridge the gap.

The right technology choices can allow close and constant communication. E-mail and data repositories can be effective for helping teams share project-related information, for example.

Interactive web conferencing and videoconferencing can be used for discussing issues, brainstorming, acknowledging accomplishments, and supporting interpersonal relationships. Company intranets can help in storing and sharing plans and other project-related documents.

While technology can assist in building and maintaining a high-performance IT team, there's no substitute for in-person meetings when it comes to solidifying relationships and focusing team effort. Building trust and motivating people are big challenges to those who manage virtual team members.

Question

Which descriptions reflect the characteristics of project team meetings?

Options:

1. Team meetings are the best forum for resolving issues and maintaining ongoing project communication
2. Team meetings should have an agenda and be facilitated to run on time and on track
3. It's important to summarize the meeting and distribute that information afterwards
4. Virtual team members should use the proper technology to participate as much as possible in team meetings
5. Technology should be used to record meetings so virtual team members don't have to attend at inconvenient times
6. Team meetings should be used to bring up personnel issues and problems with performance

Answer

Option 1: *This is a correct option. Team meetings give team members a chance to raise issues, solve problems, receive information, and develop better relationships.*

Option 2: *This is a correct option. Team meetings should be well-run to ensure that team members' time is not wasted and there's time to address all issues.*

Option 3: *This is a correct option. An important best practice for conducting team meetings is to summarize what's been accomplished and distribute meeting minutes.*

Option 4: *This is a correct option. Virtual teams, or teams with some remote members, must rely on technology during team meetings to bridge gaps caused by lack of nonverbal cues.*

Option 5: *This is an incorrect option. Technology should be used to increase personal interaction with virtual team members. A recording will have the opposite effect.*

Option 6: *This is an incorrect option. These issues should be discussed with the project manager in private. Team meetings should be about exchanging information and building personal relationships.*

3. Status reports

Consider this situation. Nico, an executive at an IT firm, is overwhelmed with paperwork on the various projects she oversees. There aren't enough hours in the day for her to read the detailed reports her project managers send her. Nico's primary concerns are whether the projects are on schedule and on track budget-wise, but in order to determine this she has to wade through multi-page reports and glean what she can. Other executives are having similar issues.

Nico isn't getting the right information. Sponsors, clients, team members, and other stakeholders need to be kept informed of project progress, but the kind of information each type of stake-holder needs about any given project can differ greatly.

Most IT project communication plans include the regular dis-tribution of a status report. Status reports are important tools for ensuring that all stakeholders receive current and accurate project information. As such, they're the most common form of written communication used in IT project management.

Status reports typically include a summary of project progress compared to schedule and cost baselines, completion of any major deliverables or milestones, and the status of outstanding issues.

Information flows from the project team to the project manager. Status reports are then used to summarize that information for the team, executive management, and other stakeholders. Sta-tus reports can be provided in a number of ways. A paper docu-ment may be circulated or an electronic document may be sent by e-mail or made accessible using a shared network folder. The method and level of detail required for each stakeholder should be specified in the communications plan.

Status reports should be customized depending upon what stakeholders are interested in. To determine what each type of status report may include, ask yourself some questions:

- What work has been accomplished since the last re-port?
- What work is scheduled during the upcoming report-ing period?
- Are there any quality or scope issues the team is con-

- cerned about?
- Is the project on budget?
- Is work proceeding on schedule?
- Do you think the project will meet its overall schedule and budget commitments?
- Do you need to make any changes to the risk assessment?

It's important to keep in mind that the goal of each status report should be to convey the state of the project to the user as clearly as possible.

Status reports should be targeted to each type of stakeholder and presented in a clear and consistent format.

Question

Which statements describe status reports and their use in IT projects?

Options:

1. Most IT projects use written status reports to keep stakeholders apprised of project progress relative to deliverables met, issues and risks, and overall adherence to schedule and budget
2. Status reports can be provided by a shared electronic folder on a network if a particular stakeholder requests this format
3. They are used to ensure all stakeholders receive the same information in exactly the same way
4. Frequently changing the format of a status report can help keep it more interesting to stakeholders who often have to wade through many such documents

Answer

Option 1: This is a correct option. Status reports are the most common form of written information used in IT project teams. Many different stakeholders can be kept up to date on project progress using them.

Option 2: This is a correct option. Status reports can be stored in a shared folder, e-mailed directly to stakeholders, or printed and distributed. The different methods can be specified in the communica-

tions plan.

Option 3: *This is an incorrect option. Not all project stakeholders require the same level of detail. For example, sponsors and team members can benefit from receiving different kinds of status reports.*

Option 4: *This is an incorrect option. Being consistent in format helps clearly put across the information about what's going on with the project. And each stakeholder will know where to find the relevant information.*

4. Project reviews

Even the most robust status reports may not be sufficient to provide the information that sponsors, clients, and executives require for high-level decision making. In those cases, organizations may use project reviews, which are formal presentations by the project manager or project team members to those responsible for organizational plans and strategies. Project reviews vary greatly in structure and content between organizations. In some organizations, project reviews may be set up on a monthly or quarterly schedule.

Preparing for a project review requires planning. As with team meetings, you'll want to develop an agenda for your presentation, decide how much time to allot to each item, and then stay focused and on track. And as in status reports, you'll want to cover major achievements for the current review period as well as issues, risks, and contingency plans. You should explain what you expect to achieve next and estimate how closely you're following your project budget and schedule.

While the information you prepare for a formal review will need to be robust, you should avoid presenting too much technical detail for your audience.

It's a good idea to prepare a high-level summary and explain the important points first.

Be prepared to give more information as executives may need you to go into greater depth on key issues.

Project reviews usually include both a verbal presentation and supplemental written information, such as handouts and slides.

Project managers typically present information to executives, although sponsors and clients may also be included. A review presented to a single type of stakeholder will be easier than one aimed at several different interested parties.

You may need to find out in advance what might be expected for the review.

Project reviews may involve more than one presenter. If you're presenting with someone from your team, you should make sure that you're both clear on the information you'll provide and the time you'll have to present the material.

Depending upon the complexity of what you're presenting and the number of people involved, it may be worthwhile to rehearse the presentation.

Job Aid

Ways to Distribute Information

Purpose: *Use this job aid for a convenient reference to the characteristics of project team meetings, status reports, and project reviews.*

Project team meetings

Project team meetings are the standard vehicle for project managers to convey information downward in an organization. Project team meetings are the best tool for resolving issues and maintaining ongoing communication.

Best practices for a well-run project team include:

- Set a regular day -- Set a regular day and time for the team meeting so team members can schedule around it.
- Emphasize attendance -- Make it clear that team members should attend or send someone else in their place.
- Distribute an agenda -- Prepare and distribute an agenda in advance.
- Start and end on time – Everyone is busy.
- Keep things on track -- Follow your agenda and use your facilitation skills to keep the meeting on track.

Encourage participation --Avoid letting a few team members monopolize the meeting and directly encourage quieter members to speak up.

- Summarize the meeting -- Wrap things up with a verbal summary of what was discussed and accomplished, and then send out written meeting minutes afterward.

Status reports

Status reports are the most common form of written communication used in IT project management.

Status reports typically include:

- a summary of project progress compared to schedule and cost baseline
- completion of any major deliverables or milestones
- the status of outstanding issues
- what work was accomplished since the last report and what is expected during the next reporting period
- any changes to the risk assessment

Project reviews

Project reviews are more formal presentations by either the project manager or project team members to executives responsible for organizational plans and strategies.

To successfully present a project review follow these tips:

- develop an agenda for your presentation
- start with a high-level summary
- decide how much time to allot to each portion
- stay focused and to the point as executives are busy people
- cover major achievements for the current review period, issues, risks, and contingency plans.
- explain what you expect to achieve for next reporting period
- estimate how closely you're following budget and schedule
- don't be excessively technical
- consider rehearsing the presentation, particularly if there is more than one presenter

Question

Which descriptions apply to project reviews and their use in IT projects?

Options:

1. Project reviews are the most common form of formal written communication in IT projects
2. Project reviews are performed by executives who gather information and prepare a report for general distribution
3. Project reviews are formal presentations by the project manager or team to those responsible for organizational management and strategy
4. Giving a project review is mandatory in IT organizations
5. Project reviews typically include information about budgets, risks, and current and planned achievements
6. When you give a project review, prepare an agenda and stay focused on the main issues

Answer

Option 1: This is an incorrect option. Status reports are the most common formal written form. Project reviews are presentations given to executives, sponsors, or clients about the project status and issues.

Option 2: This is an incorrect option. IT project reviews are presentations given by the project manager or project team at the request of executives to provide decision makers with a better idea of project status.

Option 3: This is a correct option. In project reviews, decision makers receive a formal presentation on the project and are given an opportunity to explore areas of concern more deeply.

Option 4: This is an incorrect option. Many organizations do not require formal project reviews.

Option 5: This is a correct option. Project reviews present information from the manager to the project sponsors and executives to assist in decision making.

Option 6: This option is correct. Preparing for a project review requires planning similar to that used for a team meeting. You need to create an agenda, decide how much time to allot to each portion, and then stay focused and to the point.

Question

Match each description to the appropriate method of communicating IT project information to which it applies. Each method may have more than one match.

Options:

A. The most informal type of project communication

B. A tool for updating various stakeholders on current issues

C. Often provided through a shared folder, hard copy, or e-mail

D. Often involves a project manager making a formal presentation to decision makers

E. Presented according to the level of detail required by stakeholder groups

Targets:

1. Team meetings
2. Status reports
3. Project reviews

Answer

Project team meetings keep projects on track and update information. They are the least formal way to disseminate information.

Status reports update stakeholders on project progress and the status of outstanding issues. They are usually presented in writing and are adjusted based on each stakeholder groups needs.

Project reviews are the most formal means of conveying project information. They typically involve a project manager or team members personally presenting information to decision makers.

5. Summary

Communication plays a key role in any IT project. Good communication practices can facilitate team member interaction, which improves the performance of the team, speeds up work, and saves time and money. Teams that communicate well avoid many conflicts and are in a better position to resolve the issues that do arise.

Project managers need to plan their communications carefully. A written communications plan can be a vital tool in this effort, defining communication needs, procedures, and rules. In this way, the three primary forms of project manager communications – team meetings, status reports, and formal project reviews – can be executed more effectively.

Follow-on Activity
Customized Status Reports
Purpose: *Use this activity to help you plan and practice using status reports.*
Instructions for use: Using the table provided, list the information you think should be sent to executives, functional managers, sponsors, clients, other project managers, and team members for an IT project in your company. List the detailed elements that would be part of one of the documents in the intersecting cells of the table. When you're finished filling out the table, use the information you've developed to decide how many different status reports an IT project such as this should generate. Create sample status report templates for each stakeholder type.

Status Report Information					
Executives	Functional managers	Sponsors	Clients	Other project managers	Team members

KEEPING QUALITY ON TRACK DURING IT PROJECT EXECUTION

1. Measuring quality

Consider a project manager for a company that designs voice-recognition software for business use. With their newest product, the project team would like to reach a 99% accuracy rate. After redesigning the interface and rewriting all of the code, they discover the finished product has only achieved 95%. Because it would be cost prohibitive to try to rework the code at this point, management decides to accept that rate until the next upgrade. With planning, this might have been avoided.

Quality planning is a frequently neglected aspect of project planning. Quality demands often take a backseat to cost and scheduling demands.

Project managers may think they're doing all they can by stressing quality and running their projects as efficiently as possible. But quality doesn't just happen; it must be built into project planning from the very start of an IT project.

Quality planning includes defining what quality is, what level you hope to achieve, how it will be measured, and who will be responsible. In other words, it starts with a **quality management plan.**

Quality expectations

Your project budget, the tools you have to measure quality, and how quality-oriented your company is all affect how quality is judged and achieved. Many people and factors in an organization may affect quality, but the final judges of quality are the customers and, through them, the marketplace. Project managers may also need to consider organizational standards, industry standards, and government regulations when deciding how to define high quality.

Project managers need to **define quality** in the plan in the same way customers and clients define it. Customers have expectations of reliability, maintainability, operability, and availability. The closer a product's specifications are to what users want, the more likely they are to consider it high quality.

The quality management plan should also lay out the organizational structure and clearly defined **roles and responsibilities** for quality management. Although ultimately the project manager is responsible for the final quality of the product, it may be necessary to put someone else in charge of ensuring quality during project execution and closure.

Quality management duties may be shared among several people, but someone must be in charge. The **person in charge** should keep in mind the practical tradeoffs between achieving higher quality and increased time and cost.

The quality management plan should also describe the **quality procedures** that will be performed, the processes involved, and the resources that will be needed to ensure quality. The plan should include detailed information regarding expected results and the steps that will be used to verify that standards are being met. Some of the most commonly used. methods for deciding whether quality standards are being met are **metrics**, **checklists**, and **exit criteria**.

Metrics

Quality metrics are specific and measurable characteristics related to the project quality.Each metric defines how some quality aspect of the project will be measured.

Examples of IT quality metrics include failure rate, average bandwidth, processing speed, defect rate, and memory usage.

Defining specific metrics during planning removes uncertainty in quality monitoring and testing.

Checklists

A checklist is a tool for verifying that required steps have been taken to ensure quality. As each step is completed, it's marked off the list. Checklists provide evidence that a quality control step has been taken, when it was taken, and who did the work.

A quality checklist for validating code might include a line item for "input validation is applied at all form fields" or one for "data is validated for type, length, format, and range." Whoever performed the check should sign and date the checklist.

Exit criteria

Exit criteria are checks on whether quality criteria have been met at the end of a given phase of a project. For example, the integration testing phase of a project might include exit criteria such as "The integration engineer has tested for install ability" or "All priority 1 bugs have been fixed and closed."

For the project to move into the next phase, each of these checks must be completed according to the requirements and specifications laid out in the quality management plan.

When assembling a quality management plan, remember to consider the organizational, industry, and regulatory standards that apply. Your company may have a corporate quality plan that specifies certain tools, standards, or measurements. Also, the IT industry itself has professional standards in place and some government regulations may apply. Your plan should detail how your project will ensure compliance with all of these.

2. Determining the cause of quality issues

Quality testing will tell you if you have quality issues. It may even help to determine what areas of your project are lacking quality. But measurement alone won't point you to the root causes of problems. There are many special tools for determining the sources of quality issues. Three important ones are

cause-and-effect diagrams, Pareto analysis, and **peer reviews.**
Cause-and-effect diagrams, also known as Ishikawa diagrams, are one of the most useful tools for determining the sources of quality problems. Based on the premise that every output problem has one or more input variables, the step-by-step construction of this diagram can help pinpoint the actual cause of the output problem in some cases.

Select the steps for using a cause-and-effect diagram in order to learn more about how this tool helps you drill down and pinpoint the input variables that cause an output problem.

Statement of the problem

The cause-and-effect diagram process is usually conducted in a single informal brainstorming meeting. Team members combine their energy and insights to come up with a wide-ranging list of potential input factors.

You begin the diagram by placing a statement of the quality problem in the box on the right. The main branches are then filled in with the elements of the system that may be causing the problem. In general, these fall into three main categories: conditions, events, and actions.

Find cause variables

Now your team takes the second step of determining possible causes. The group writes down all the brainstorming ideas that come to mind. Procedures, people, processes, or tools that are potential causes are listed on the smaller branches. Issues that seem related are grouped together.

The finished shape of the cause-and-effect diagram gives it its other common name – the fishbone diagram.

Narrow to likely causes

The team now narrows down all the possible causes to the few that seem most likely, and then tests and verifies the results to validate which are the true causes of the quality issues.

Kylie's IT team is working on improving a wireless phone system. At the team meeting, Kylie draws a line and a box on the whiteboard. In the box, she puts a statement of the problem: "High rate of dropped calls."

Everyone at the meeting is given a pad of sticky notes for jotting down ideas. The sticky notes are to be attached to the appropriate places on the diagram as the session progresses. Kylie asks everyone to think of all the different elements of the system that could be affecting the rate of dropped calls. She labels the main branches of the diagram with these key elements.

After the team has exhausted ideas for the elements, Kylie asks them to come up with all the possible causes of each element.

In Kylie's case, the team decides that the most likely causes are related to the system hardware.

They do further testing and determine the system is not overloaded, but there is an incorrect connection.

The cause-and-effect diagram pointed the team at the root cause of the issue.

The second tool for determining the source of a quality problem is **Pareto analysis**. Pareto analysis is based on the Pareto Principle or 80/20 rule, which states that approximately 20% of the issues cause 80% of the problems in any given situation. Not all data will fall neatly into this pattern, but most will. Charting your data using a Pareto chart can make clear the top two or three categories into which the majority of your problems fall.

A Pareto chart is a specialized form of histogram – the common graph for showing how often each unique value in a set of data occurs. Instead of grouping results by intervals as in histograms, Pareto charts lump similar quality issues together into categories to identify problem areas. Pareto analysis requires three steps: **construct a frequency distribution**, **create a Pareto chart**, and **analyze results**.

Construct a frequency distribution

Assemble a frequency distribution for the various categories of problems you can identify. For an IT project, you may want to classify problems as code related, hardware related, interface related, or operating system related, for example.

Collect the data – a count of each error – in a correct and consistent manner.

Create a Pareto chart

Turn the frequency distribution into a Pareto chart by labeling the horizontal axis as the categories and the vertical axis as the frequency or counted value. Now you graph the frequencies as bars, placed side by side.

The height of each bar represents the percentage of problems caused by that category. The largest bar should go on the left, and you should place the remaining bars in descending order of height so that the smallest bar falls on the right.

Analyze results

If your data follows the Pareto Principle, the chart should show that the majority of your problems fall into the first two or three categories. If this is the case with your chart, start on the left and identify which categories make up approximately 80% of your quality issues. Then focus your correction efforts on these categories to reduce the overall number of errors.

You may want to create Pareto charts within those categories to drill down and attempt to identify the roots of the problems.

So in a Pareto diagram, the columns depict the types or sources of problems and the scale on the left shows the frequency – the number of times that type of problem occurs.

A Pareto diagram does not by itself identify the cause of a particular problem. But it can make the critical issues that cause your quality problems more obvious.

By focusing on those causes, you can resolve or reduce some of them and perhaps get a better idea of what's really happening. Other analytical tools may be used in conjunction with Pareto diagrams to identify root causes.

Remember Kylie? Her team decides to use a Pareto analysis to search for the source of the problem. She begins by gathering data for a frequency distribution.

She then takes the percentages she has calculated from the frequency distribution and creates a Pareto chart. The chart has bars showing the major areas where errors occur and what percentage of errors falls within each category.

In most cases, two or three causes – or categories of causes – will tower above the others. So you must look for a break point in the cumulative percentage line. This point occurs where the slope of the line begins to flatten out. The causes under the steepest part of the curve are the most important because it's these that account for the bulk of the problems. They are the high-impact causes on which you need to focus.

Next you drop a line down to the x-axis from the break point. This defines a square or rectangular shape on the chart. Any causes that fall to the left of your vertical line are responsible for 80% of the recorded errors or problems.

The Pareto diagram tells Kylie which of the causes to focus on and how much benefit she will obtain by tackling and resolving each root cause. Together, system hardware and software problems account for 80% of all errors. The cause of the dropped call problem is likely to be found in those areas.

A third valuable tool in determining the cause of quality problems is **peer review**. A peer review is an assessment of work conducted by another person on the team.

By getting team members to comment on each other's requirements, design, and code, you can leverage the expertise and knowledge of your team to identify problems early and improve the quality of the product.

In many organizations, peer reviews are mandated for software development as part of the validation process.

Job Aid

Quality Management Tools

Purpose: *Use this job aid for a convenient reference to the tools available to help project managers ensure quality.*

Cause-and-effect diagrams

Cause-and-effect diagrams, also known as Ishikawa diagrams, are one of the most useful tools for determining the sources of quality problems.

To use a cause-and-effect diagram:

- **State the problem** -- Begin the diagram by placing a statement of the quality problem in the box at the right of the diagram.
- **Brainstorm elements** –Have team members brainstorm all the possible elements of the system that could affect the issue.
- **Fill main branches** – Fill in the main branches with the elements of the system that may be causing the problem.
- **Brainstorm causes** –Have team members brainstorm all the possible causes under each element.
- **Fill contributing branches** – List potential causes the smaller branches
- **Narrow things down** -- Narrow down all the possible causes to the few that seem most likely
- **Keep things on track** -- Test and verifies to validate which are the true causes of the quality issues.

Pareto analysis

A Pareto chart is a specialized form of histogram that groups similar quality issues together into categories in order to identify the areas that need corrective action. The analysis is based on the 80/20 rule that says approximately 20 percent of the issues cause 80 percent of the problems in any given situation.

To use Pareto analysis:

- assemble a frequency distribution for the various categories of problems you can identify.
- construct a Pareto chart of the distribution by labeling the horizontal axis as the categories and the vertical axis as the frequency or counted value.
- graph the frequencies as bars, placed side by side.
- if your chart follows the Pareto principle, identify

which categories make up approximately 80% of your quality issues and focus your correction efforts on these categories to reduce the overall amount of error.

Peer reviews

A peer review is an assessment of work conducted by another person on the team.

To use peer reviews for managing quality:

- assign team members to comment on each other's requirements, design, or code at various points in the process

Some team members have different skill sets and experience than others, and may be able to spot problems before they become cost prohibitive to fix. If the product being assessed is source code, for example, have other programmers on the team perform the review. Peer reviews may work to reduce cosmetic issues related to internal standards such as indentation and variable naming conventions. They may also identify issues related to the efficiency of the programming or even more severe items.

Question

Match each of the quality management tools to its description.

Options:

A. Cause-and-effect diagram
B. Pareto analysis
C. Peer review

Targets:

1. Also known as a fishbone diagram, use of this tool requires that the team brainstorm the sources of quality problems, identify contributing elements, and then examine each element more closely for possible causes

2. Based on the 80/20 rule, this tool uses a frequency distribution and chart to identify the few critical problem areas that cause the majority of issues

3. Quality management tool that leverages the expertise of teammates to perform checks on fellow team mem-

bers' work

Answer

Cause-and-effect diagrams are also known as Ishikawa diagrams or fishbone diagrams. They're based on brainstorming by team members who chart the possible cause-and-effect variables they can identify and then narrow down the likely causes.

Pareto analysis is a quality management tool that uses data compiled in a frequency distribution to produce a specialized histogram. The chart makes obvious which few factors are responsible for the vast majority of errors.

Peer reviews make use of fellow team members' skills and expertise by having teammates formally review each other's work.

3. Summary

Just as with communications, ensuring quality is a vital component of project execution that deserves planning and effort from project managers. A written quality management plan should be developed that spells out objectives, roles, and responsibilities. It should also establish the quality standards and procedures – such as metrics, checklists, and exit criteria – that will be used to ensure quality.

When defects or problems arise, it's important to be able to trace them back to their root causes. Several common tools can help including cause-and-effect diagrams, Pareto analysis, and peer reviews. Project managers are ultimately responsible for managing the quality of projects.

IT PROJECT MANAGEMENT ESSENTIALS: MONITORING AND CONTROLLING IT PROJECTS

Managing IT projects is a difficult and demanding task. They can be complex, with many variables, and the project manager needs to know what is happening in every job and task involved in the project. With so much to concentrate on and the high potential for it to go wrong, a project manager could be compared to an entertainer trying to juggle and walk a tightrope at the same time.

The project manager needs to be able to survey all aspects of the project and generate data that will help gauge progress. In this course, you will learn how to achieve control of even the most complex IT projects by using the correct processes. Learning how to monitor and control an IT project is the key aim of this course.

This course will also explain how to analyze the variances that can occur in a project and use this information to assess and recommend actions that may need to be taken to ensure the project remains on track.

The course demonstrates how to deal with proposed changes to a project. This can be achieved by negotiating the five steps of the change control process.

Monitoring and Controlling IT Projects
1. Monitoring the Progress of an IT Project
2. Analyzing Variances in an IT Project
3. Controlling Changes to IT Projects

MONITORING THE PROGRESS OF AN IT PROJECT

1. Project monitoring and control

An unsupervised project can quickly careen out of control. If a project manager isn't mindful of the variances that can occur during every stage of the project, a potentially costly error may occur. Project managers can be likened to navigators, pilots, or captains of a boat in that they need to ensure a project remains on course.

This safeguarding of a project from inception to completion is the role of project managers. They must try their best to ensure that the project is completed within the constraints outlined at its start. They must also achieve each objective outlined in the project plan. These objectives provide the path for the project to follow.

Project monitoring and control are key in assessing how the project is progressing - that is, what stage the project is at and what stage the project is supposed to be at.

So project monitoring compares the actual performance of a project with the planned or expected performance of the project. The monitoring process assesses trends based on collated performance data. It also contributes to the development of forecasts concerning future cost and schedule performance.

Monitoring is closely linked with project control. The results derived from monitoring give the project manager the details required to control the direction of the project. The controlling process then analyzes variances in performance. It seeks to evaluate alternative means and actions, which could bring a wayward project's performance back in line with its original plan. Project control involves identifying and recommending actions that can either be preventive or corrective, depending on a particular situation.

It's essential that monitoring and control are carried out for the duration of a project. They are of equal importance for the planning, execution, and closing stages of a project.

The baseline, or the planned performance, is used to help monitor a project. The baseline is the final approved plan for a project. It is signed off on by senior management or the customer once all necessary changes are made to the plan.

Different parts of a project plan will have their own individual baselines, which are incorporated in the overall plan. For example, the baseline for time is the schedule, and the baseline for cost is the budget. And the baseline for scope is the Work Breakdown Structure (WBS).

A project's baseline will not be changed to match the actual progress of a project. Changes can only be made to the baseline if an approved change request is made. This could happen if circumstances dictate that the project's schedule needs to be delayed or brought forward. Another situation where the baseline could be changed is if the baseline differs from the actual progress to such an extent that there is no benefit from comparing the two.

Question

How are the processes of monitoring and control linked?

Options:

1. They both involve the comparison of the actual performance of the project with the planned or expected performance of the project
2. The results of monitoring provide the project manager with the details required to control the direction of the project
3. The controlling process shapes how a project is monitored during its life cycle

Answer

Option 1: *This option is incorrect. Monitoring is focused on the actual performance of the project with the planned or expected performance. Controlling uses that information to decide what action to take if a change is required to get the project back on track.*

Option 2: *This is the correct option. The monitoring process determines how well the project is progressing according to expectations. The results of this process feed into the control process. If a change needs to be made to get the project back on track, the control process kicks in to evaluate options and decide on the best course of action.*

Option 3: *This is an incorrect option. The controlling process analyzes variances that are identified during monitoring. It seeks to evaluate alternative means and actions, which could bring a wayward project's performance back in line with its original plan.*

2. Earned value management

The monitoring of a project is often carried out using earned value management (EVM). This is a term that is applied to, and describes, the general application of earned value analysis (EVA) to monitoring a project's progress. Earned value analysis is a technique that uses work–in–progress data to indicate what is likely to happen to work relating to a project in the future. It tracks the progress of a project against actual accomplishment, using the WBS budget and schedule estimates.

Earned value is defined by the Project Management Body of Knowledge (PMBOK) as the value of the work that has been completed based on the budget for that work.

Earned value analysis differs from more traditional progress measurement techniques. Its advantage lies in the fact that it measures actual accomplishment.

Earned value analysis incorporates scope, cost, and time into its measurements. By integrating these, EVA clarifies and provides a current assessment of a project's progress.

Project management professionals are often reluctant to use earned value analysis because they perceive that the calculations it requires are too difficult. But by opting not to use this type of analysis, they are missing out on significant benefits in terms of tracking a project's progress.

The first way that earned value analysis allows a project manager to better manage a project is by integrating cost, schedule, and scope performance. Analyzing these elements in an integrated way provides a clear situation report concerning the project's progress.

The second benefit of using earned value analysis is that it can be used to forecast future performances and project completion dates. This forecasting is very useful and contributes to the better management of current and future projects in terms of completing them on time, and within budget.

The third benefit arising from using earned value analysis to track project progress is that it acts as an early warning system that allows managers to identify and control problems before they become insurmountable. By identifying problems at an early stage, a project manager can prevent substantial overruns in the budget and help keep the project focused and on schedule.

The final benefit is that it gives project managers insight into potential risk areas. This previewing of potential risks allows project managers to take appropriate action to avoid the risks by creating risk mitigation plans based on the cost, schedule, and progress of the project.

Question

What are the benefits of using earned value analysis (EVA) to track project progress?

Options:

1. EVA integrates cost, schedule, and scope performance
2. EVA can forecast future performance and project completion dates
3. EVA provides early warning of potential problems
4. EVA provides insight into potential risk areas
5. EVA ensures that the project is delivered on time and within budget
6. EVA removes the element of uncertainty from a project

Answer

Option 1: *This option is correct. By integrating cost, schedule, and scope performance, EVA provides an accurate picture of a project's progress.*

Option 2: *This option is correct. By forecasting future performance and project completion dates, EVA provides very useful data for project managers.*

Option 3: *This option is correct. The early warning of potential problems, which EVA provides, helps project managers to plan ahead.*

Option 4: *This option is correct. Gaining an insight into potential risk areas is a benefit of using EVA. This early indicator can help avoid costly mistakes during the project.*

Option 5: *This option is incorrect. EVA is a progress monitoring technique and can only be used to generate information a project manager uses. EVA cannot be used to ensure that a project is delivered on time and within budget.*

Option 6: *This option is incorrect. EVA cannot be used to remove the element of uncertainty from a project. All projects are vulnerable to unknown elements.*

3. Earned value analysis calculations

To understand and use earned value analysis, it's necessary to become familiar with the three terms it uses. The terms are planned value (PV), actual cost (AC), and work performed (EV).

Planned value (PV)

Planned value is the budget for the work scheduled for the project. It is sometimes referred to as budgeted cost of work scheduled (BCWS). Think of planned value as the total amount of funding for the expected or scheduled work to be carried out for the duration of the project.

For each task within the project, there is a planned value. The total budgeted cost for the project is the sum of all these individual planned values added together.

Actual cost (AC)

Actual cost is the amount of money that is actually spent to fully complete the project. This figure includes the cost of labor and material, as well as vendor and subcontractor costs. Actual cost is also known as actual cost of work performed (ACWP).

Work performed (EV)

Work performed is also referred to as earned value (EV) in calculations referring to earned value analysis. It is also known as budgeted cost of work performed (BCWP). Work performed represents the value of the actual work completed and compared against the planned or budgeted amount for that period.

To calculate the PV, AC, and EV for a project, you need to begin with a status date. In this example, the status date is the end of February. The project in question involves four separate tasks. Task A begins in January, and is expected to take one month to complete. It has a budget of $5,000. Task B begins in January, and is expected to finish at the end of February. It has a budget of $10,000.

Task C begins in February, and is expected to be complete at the end of March. Its budget is $20,000.

Task D begins in April, and is expected to be finished at the end of May. It has a budget of $10,000.

In order to carry out the necessary calculations, a project manager will need to know some more details. Given that the status date is the end of February, the project manager needs to know how much actual work has been completed for each task, and also how much it has cost to carry out this work up until the end of February.

At the end of February, Task A is 100% complete and the cost is $6,000. And Task B is 80% complete and the cost is $11,000. Meanwhile, Task C is 20% complete and the cost is $30,000.

Task D commenced after the status date, so it won't be involved in the calculations.

To calculate the PV for the project, add together the budgeted costs of the three tasks - in this case, Task A is $5,000, Task B is $10,000, and Task C is $20,000. But because the status date is only half way through the scheduled time for Task C, only half the budgeted cost, $10,000, is added. This means that the PV for the project up until the end of February is $25,000.

To calculate the EV, add together the amounts that have been earned. For Task A, 100% of the money, $5,000, has been earned. Only 80% of Task B has been earned, which is $8,000. For Task C, 20% has been earned, which amounts to $4,000. The EV works out as $17,000.

To calculate the AC, add together the real amount the work for each task has cost up until the end of February. Task A cost $6,000, Task B cost $11,000, and Task C cost $30,000. This means that the AC is $47,000.

Question

A project to outfit a newly built office block with the necessary IT equipment involves four separate jobs. Job A is due to begin in June and finish at the end of July. It's budgeted to cost $10,000. Job B is due to begin in June and set to be completed by the end of the month. Its budget is $4,000. Job C is set to begin in June and be completed by the end of July. Its budget is $60,000. And Job D is due to begin in August and set to be completed by the end of September with a budget of $15,000. The status date for the assessment of the project is the end of July.

By the end of July, Job A is 80% complete and has cost $12,000. Job B is 100% complete and has cost $8,000. Job C is 60% complete and costs $70,000. Match PV, EV, and AC to the figures they represent.

Options:

    A.   PV

    B.   EV

    C.   AC

Targets:

1. $74,000
2. $48,000
3. $90,000

Answer

The PV for this project is the sum of Job A's budget, $10,000, plus Job B's budget, $4,000, plus Job C's budget, $60,000. Job D isn't part of

these calculations as the assessment status date is the end of July.
The EV for this project is the sum of the earned money for the
three projects. For Job A 80% of $10,000 was earned, which equals
$8,000. For Job B 100% of $4,000 was earned. For Job C 60% of
$60,000 was earned, which is $36,000.
The AC for this project is the sum of the actual cost for the three jobs.
Job A cost $12,000, Job B cost $8,000, and Job C cost $70,000.

4. Cost and schedule variance

Using variance management techniques to control a project is
very effective. Earned value analysis provides the data needed to
calculate variance.

The calculations for planned value (PV), actual cost (AC), and
work performed (EV) can be used to determine whether or not
the cost and the schedule is varying from the project's baseline.

Variance management determines the acceptable level of variance from the planned budget and schedule that can be tolerated.

When project managers refer to budget variance, they are talking about the difference between the amount originally allocated to the budget and the actual costs the project has incurred
so far.

This calculation is called cost variance, or CV.

To calculate the CV of a project, subtract the project's actual
cost, or AC, from the work performed, or EV. A positive variance means that the project is saving money. A negative variance
means the project is running over budget and requires immediate corrective action.

A similar situation applies in terms of schedule. Schedule variance, or SV, is the difference between a project's actual progress
– EV – and its estimated progress – PV. This calculation is represented in terms of cost. A positive variance means the project is
ahead of schedule, and a negative variance means the project is
behind schedule.

An IT management company wins a contract to create a new
network architecture for a bank that is eager to replace its legacy

systems. Two months after the project commences, the project manager carries out some calculations. The PV for the project is $30,000. The AC is $40,000, and the EV is $50,000.

The project manager calculates the cost variance for the project. She subtracts the AC of $40,000 from the EV of $50,000. So, the variance in cost is $10,000. She also calculates the SV for the project. To do this, she subtracts the PV of $30,000 from the EV of $50,000. Therefore, the SV is $20,000. Because both the CV and SV are positive, the project is under budget and ahead of schedule.

Question

If the EV, AC, and PV for an IT project are $70,000, $65,000, and $57,000 respectively, which figure represents the project's CV and which figure represents the project's SV?

Options:

A.   CV

B.   SV

Targets:

1. $5,000
2. $13,000

Answer

The CV for the project is calculated by subtracting the AC of $65,000 from the EV of $70,000.

The SV for the project is calculated by subtracting the PV of $57,000 from the EV of $70,000.

Project managers use indexes to create ratios between both a project's budgetary components and scheduling components. These indexes, which use earned value analysis, can tell a project manager whether she will have enough funds to finish the budget, or enough time left to finish it on schedule.

If the calculated ratio is greater than 1, the project is ahead of schedule or under budget.

If the ratio is less than 1, the project is behind schedule or over budget.

The first of these performance indexes is called the cost performance index, or CPI which is the quotient of the EV and the

AC. This means it shows the rate at which the project performance is meeting cost expectations during a given period of time. CPI is a critical EVM metric because it tells you how the project is really performing in terms of cost.

The second performance index is the schedule performance index, or SPI, which is the quotient of EV and PV. In other words, it indicates how the value of performed work compares to the value of planned work.

Because these indexes predict how much extra time or money might be needed to finish a project, they are more useful than variance calculations to convey a project's progress to stakeholders. Both the CPI and SPI indicators deliver an accurate portrayal of a project's health.

In the example of the IT project to create a new network architecture for a bank, the PV for the project is $30,000, the AC is $40,000, and the EV is $50,000. The project manager is asked to generate a status report and decides to incorporate performance indexes.

First, she calculates the SPI by dividing the EV of $50,000 by the PV of $30,000. The SPI is 1.67. As the SPI is greater than one, the project is ahead of schedule. She then calculates the CPI by dividing the EV of $50,000 by the AC of $40,000. The CPI is 1.25. A CPI value higher than one indicates that a project is earning more than is being spent. A value lower than one indicates a cost overrun. A CPI of 1.25 indicates that the project is getting $1.25 for every dollar spent.

Question

Match the term to its corresponding description.

Options:

A.   Cost variance (CV)
B.   Schedule variance (SV)
C.   Cost performance index (CPI)
D.   Schedule performance index (SPI)

Targets:

1. The difference between a project's allocated budget and the actual costs the project has incurred

2. The difference between a project's actual progress and its estimated progress
3. The ratio between a project's budgeted costs and actual costs
4. The ratio between work performed on a project and the work that was scheduled

Answer

Cost variance is the difference between a project's allocated budget and the actual costs the project has incurred. It is calculated by subtracting the AC from the EV.

Schedule variance is the difference between a project's actual progress and its estimated progress. To calculate SV, subtract a project's PV from its EV.

The cost performance index is the ratio between a project's budgeted costs and actual costs. To calculate CPI, divide a project's EV by its AC.

The schedule performance index is the ratio between work performed on a project and the work that was scheduled. To calculate the SPI, divide a project's EV by its PV.

Case Study: Question 1 of 3

Scenario

For your convenience, the case study is repeated with each question.

Now use the terms to calculate variance for a sample project. An insurance company hires an IT project management firm to oversee the implementation of a real-time pensions and policies processing system application for its web site. The work completed for the project is $25,000. The actual cost is $35,000, and the planned value is $17,000.

Determine the cost variance (CV), schedule variance (SV), cost performance index (CPI), and schedule performance index (SPI) for the project.

Question

What is the cost variance (CV) for the project?

Options:

1. -$10,000

2. $8,000
3. $60,000

Answer

Option 1: *This is the correct option. To calculate the CV for the project, subtract its AC of $35,000 from its EV of $25,000.*

Option 2: *This option is incorrect. To calculate the CV for the project, subtract its AC of $35,000 from its EV of $25,000. You may have mistaken the PV for the AC.*

Option 3: *This option is incorrect. Remember, to calculate the CV for the project, subtract its AC of $35,000 from its EV of $25,000. Here, the figures were added together to come up with $60,000.*

Case Study: Question 2 of 3

Scenario

For your convenience, the case study is repeated with each question.
Now use the terms to calculate variance for a sample project. An insurance company hires an IT project management firm to oversee the implementation of a real-time pensions and policies processing system application for its web site. The work completed for the project is $25,000. The actual cost is $35,000, and the planned value is $17,000.

Determine the cost variance (CV), schedule variance (SV), cost performance index (CPI), and schedule performance index (SPI) for the project.

Question

What is the schedule variance (SV) for the project?

Options:

1. $8,000
2. $10,000
3. 8 hours

Answer

Option 1: *This is the correct option. To calculate the SV for the project, subtract the PV of $17,000 from the EV of $25,000.*

Option 2: *This option is incorrect. You may have made a miscalculation. To calculate the SV for the project, subtract the PV of $17,000 from the EV of $25,000.*

Option 3: *This option is incorrect. Remember, schedule variance is represented in terms of cost. In order to calculate the SV for the project, subtract the PV of $17,000 from the EV of $25,000.*

Case Study: Question 3 of 3
Scenario
For your convenience, the case study is repeated with each question.
Now use the terms to calculate variance for a sample project. An insurance company hires an IT project management firm to oversee the implementation of a real-time pensions and policies processing system application for its web site. The work completed for the project is $25,000. The actual cost is $35,000, and the planned value is $17,000.
Determine the cost variance (CV), schedule variance (SV), cost performance index (CPI), and schedule performance index (SPI) for the project.
Question
Match the cost performance index (CPI) and schedule performance (SPI) index to their corresponding figures. Please round figures to two decimal places.
Options:
    A.   Cost performance index (CPI)
    B.   Schedule performance index (SPI)
Targets:
    1. 0.71
    2. 1.47
Answer
The cost performance index for the project is calculated by dividing the EV of $25,000 by the AC of $35,000. A CPI of 0.71 indicates a cost overrun and that the project is getting only 70 cents for every dollar spent.
The schedule performance index for the project is calculated by dividing the EV of $25,000 by the PV of $17,000. An SPI value greater than one tells you that a project is ahead of its planned schedule. A value less than one indicates poor performance.

5. Summary

Project monitoring and control are two key elements in overseeing a project. Project monitoring involves the comparison of the actual performance of the project with the planned or expected performance of the project. Project control is closely linked with monitoring. The controlling process analyzes variances in performance.

The monitoring of a project is often carried out using earned value management (EVM) and earned value analysis (EVA). Earned value analysis involves terms such as planned value (PV), actual cost (AC), work performed (EV), cost variance (CV), and schedule variance (SV). Indexes are also used in earned value analysis: the cost performance index (CPI) and the schedule performance index (SPI).

Job Aid

Project Monitoring Terms

Purpose: *Use this job aid to review the terms associated with project monitoring.*

Actual cost (AC)
Work performed (EV)
Planned value (PV)
Cost variance (CV)
Schedule variance (SV)
Cost performance index (CPI)

ANALYZING VARIANCES IN AN IT PROJECT

1. Analyzing variances in performance

Understanding variances is something most people do everyday. Take an amateur athlete preparing for her first marathon. She creates an exercise plan in advance, and will work toward the goals it outlines. She'll know that by week two, she should be running at least 15 miles per week. If she's running more or less than that, she'll know that she should either work harder to reach the target or reduce her work to hit the target without getting burned out.

This analysis of variance in her performance allows her to control her future progress and finish the marathon.

Similarly, for a project manager to retain control over an IT project, he must be able to analyze variances in performance.

These variances, once properly interpreted, can provide information about the project's critical needs.

When variance management is applied to IT projects, the project manager can use the variance data to determine what measures may need to be taken to keep the project focused.

To analyze variances in performance, a project manager will first need to consider how close each task, job, or component involved in the project is to the original plan, in terms of schedule and cost.

It's important that projects are kept as close as possible to their original plans so that they can be recovered if they stray off course.

That's why boundaries are established in project plans. These boundaries form the acceptable level of variance that can be tolerated in the project. A general acknowledgement in project management is that a project can only tolerate variance from its original budget or schedule in the region of 10%. If a project varies by more than 15%, it can only ever be brought back to within 10% of the original plan. This is why constant monitoring and control are so crucial.

At various points throughout project execution, project managers can use performance indexes to establish an accurate progress report for the project in question.

Both the schedule performance index, SPI, and the cost performance index, CPI, are used to determine how close a project is to its original plan and how near the budget or schedule is to the boundaries established in the original plan.

If the SPI and CPI are greater than one, then the project is healthy. If the indexes are less than one, there's a problem with the project that needs to be addressed.

Setting lower limit boundaries

Project managers sometimes wonder why it's necessary to set a lower limit boundary, particularly where budget is concerned. It's because there are issues that need to be considered if a project is running under budget, such as whether tasks are being fully completed or not.

Question

What does a project manager need to do in order to analyze how close each task in a project is to its plan?

Options:

1. Establish the accepted boundaries of variance the task can tolerate
2. Accept that around 10% is the maximum permitted level of variance from the original plan
3. Use SPI and CPI to help analyze performance of the task

4. Consider whether the task can be dropped from the schedule
5. Compare the task to a similar one from another project

Answer

Option 1: *This option is correct. By establishing the accepted boundaries of variance the task can tolerate, the project manager is setting useful parameters that can indicate if a project is in trouble.*

Option 2: *This option is correct. By accepting that roughly 10% is the maximum permitted level of variance from the original plan, the project manager is keeping close control of the task and will be able to make modifications to get the task back on course if necessary.*

Option 3: *This option is correct. Using SPI and CPI to help analyze performance allows the project manager to accurately track a task's performance.*

Option 4: *This option is incorrect. At this point, the tasks on your schedule are ones that need to be carried out. So you wouldn't want to drop anything.*

Option 5: *This option is incorrect. Comparing the task to a similar one from another project is something you might do at the planning stages. But now you need to analyze data relating to a task's progress.*

2. Earned value calculations

In addition to knowing how close each task is to its plan, project managers also need to determine how the present project status – if it's out of control – will impact the future project status if they want to keep control of their projects. If the SPI or CPI of a project shows that it's straying beyond control, the project manager will need to know how to forecast and analyze the variances. This analysis can be facilitated by using earned value calculations.

The first type of earned value calculation is called estimate at completion, or EAC. The second is known as the estimate to complete, or ETC. To calculate both EAC and ETC, you'll first need to determine the budget at completion also known as BAC. The BAC is the total budget of the project.

EAC is a very important figure for project managers, senior management, and shareholders as it gives you a more realistic idea of future project performance than the BAC. It's nearly always expected to feature in any project's status report. EAC enables you to forecast and estimate what the total cost of completing a project will be, based on its performance so far.

To calculate the EAC for a project, you need to know the budget at completion and the cost performance index. The BAC is determined by adding together the planned value (PV for short) for each task or job involved in the project. The CPI is determined by dividing the value of the actual work completed – the EV – by the actual cost – the AC.

Once you have these figures, you divide the BAC by the CPI to get the EAC.

The second earned value calculation, ETC, provides the estimated amount of money required to complete the project. ETC is used by project managers, senior management, and financial comptrollers to determine the cash flow that will be required until the project has finished.

To calculate the ETC for a project, subtract the AC from the determined EAC.

Question

Match the earned value calculation to its formula.

Options:

    A.   Estimate at completion, or EAC

    B.   Estimate to complete, or ETC

Targets:

    1. Budget at completion, or BAC, divided by the cost performance index, or CPI

    2. Estimate at Completion or EAC, minus the actual cost, or AC

Answer

To calculate the EAC, you divide the budget at completion by the cost performance index.

To calculate the ETC, you subtract the actual cost from the estimate at completion.

Consider this example of calculating the EAC for a project to install backup servers in a data center. The BAC for the project has been calculated at $25,000. The CPI is 0.79, which is the value of the actual work completed - $11,500, in this case - divided by its actual cost of $14,500.

To calculate the EAC, the project manager divides the BAC of $25,000 by the CPI of 0.79. The EAC is $31,645.57.

The new EAC is larger than the BAC by more than $6,000. This is quite a lot and requires the project manager's immediate attention.

To calculate the ETC for the backup servers project, the project manager subtracts the AC of $14,500 from the EAC of $31,645.57. The ETC is $17,145.57. This is the amount of money needed to finish the project.

Question

A project manager is asked to produce a progress report for a job that involves the creation of new in-house software for database management. The BAC for the project is $45,000, the AC is $32,000, and the CPI is 0.92.

Match the terms to the figures that represent them.

Options:

    A.   EAC

    B.   ETC

Targets:

    1. $48,913.04

    2. $16,913.04

Answer

To calculate the EAC for the project, divide the BAC of $45,000 by the CPI of 0.92.

To calculate the ETC for the project, subtract the AC of $32,000 from the predetermined EAC of $48,913.04.

Question

A networking solutions provider has received a contract to establish the infrastructure for a company's wide area network.

The BAC for the project is $500,000, the AC is $55,000, and the CPI is 1.09.

Match the terms to the figures that represent them.
Options:
    A.   EAC
    B.   ETC
Targets:
    1. $458,715.59
    2. $403,715.59

Answer

To calculate the EAC for the project, divide the BAC of $500,000 by the CPI of 1.09.

To calculate the ETC for the project, subtract the AC of $55,000 from the EAC of $458,715.59.

The information provided by the EAC and ETC is needed to assess and recommend actions that may be needed to keep a project on track. Variances will almost inevitably occur during a project. But their occurrence in a project doesn't necessarily indicate that the project is in trouble. It will be the project manager who will have to collate and assess the data, and determine whether or not corrective action is required.

Question

If a project manager wants to determine how present status will impact the future project status, what should she do?

Options:
1. If the CPI or SPI, or both, indicate the project is out of control, analyze what the variances mean
2. Calculate the new estimate at project's completion using the CPI and the budget at completion
3. Let the project run its natural course and then evaluate the data
4. Stop all aspects of the project until the necessary calculations are made
5. Figure out how much money will be needed to com-

plete the project

Answer

Option 1: *This option is correct. If the CPI or SPI, or both indicate the project is out of control, the project manager needs to analyze what the variances mean.*

Option 2: *This option is correct. By using earned value calculations, such as that for a new estimate at project's completion, the project manager will be able to achieve a better understanding of how much the variance will affect the project's progress.*

Option 3: *This option is incorrect. Letting the project run its natural course and then evaluating the data is a reckless approach to project management.*

Option 4: *This option is incorrect. Stopping all aspects of the project until the necessary calculations are made is counterproductive and would compromise the accuracy of the data.*

Option 5: *This option is correct. Calculating the EAC or estimate at completion will help the project manager determine what to do about a variance. If it's unacceptable, action will need to be taken.*

3. Summary

If a project manager wants to retain control over an IT project, he must be able to analyze variances in performance. These variances can provide information about the project's critical needs. Project managers use performance indexes to establish an accurate progress report for the project in question. Both the schedule performance index (SPI) and the cost performance index (CPI) are used to determine how close a project is to its original plan.

Project managers also need to determine how the present project status – if out of control – will impact the future project status. Earned value (forecasting) calculations are used to achieve this. The first type of earned value calculation is called the estimate at completion, or EAC, and the second is known as estimate to complete, or ETC.

CONTROLLING CHANGES TO IT PROJECTS

1. The change control process

Every aspect of a prospective project can be planned and measured in great detail. Schedules and budgets are established and resources are sourced. Uncertainty and doubt are removed from the plan as much as is possible. All is fine until the project actually begins, and then the problems may arise and changes may need to be made to the project plan. Despite the best preparation and planning, all projects experience this need for change to some degree.

IT projects are particularly susceptible to change. This is because of the complex nature of many IT projects and the constant upgrading of hardware and software. Project managers accept that change is inevitable and use a change control process to manage it. Any request made during the course of the project that adds new requirements or expands the scope of a project must go through the established change control process.

There are many reasons for a change to be requested during a project. It could be as simple as the customer deciding that the project's deliverables need to incorporate another element. Or half way through the project, a team member discovers that the software that is being implemented isn't able to deliver the project's goals, or it isn't compatible with existing software. Perhaps the software becomes outdated during the course of the installation.

Project managers need to be aware of the categories or types of changes that may need to be implemented during the course of a project. For example, some changes are initiated by the customer as a result of the project's needs being re-evaluated.

Another type of change that can occur in a project includes alterations that become necessary as the project develops.

The changes initiated by the customer are often necessary because the project requirements were not properly defined at the outset, or the technology involved becomes outdated. These changes are increasingly likely to happen with an IT project involving new or developing technology.

In this case, the project requirements can't be adequately defined until a certain amount of prototyping and testing is carried out. These changes affect the scope of the project.

The second set of changes a project could face arises as the project proceeds. Changes in this category are internal to the project and are identified by the project team rather than suggested by a customer. These changes often constitute enhancements that the design and development processes have identified as being necessary for the project to continue. These changes may, or may not require the project's scope to be amended.

To deal with changes you have encountered or may encounter on your projects, you need to implement a change control process.

This is a documented process for proposing, reviewing, and allowing – or refusing – changes within a project. Such a process allows you to review changes in terms of their value, costs, impact on schedule, feasibility, and risks.

A properly implemented change control process assesses the impact the change will have on a project. A project manager can use the change control process to manage status updates arising from changes, and ensure the necessary actions are taken to accommodate the changes throughout the relevant areas of the project plan.

The change control process can be broken down into different subsections, each of which deals with a certain aspect of the project. These include scope change control, schedule control, cost control, quality control, and risk control.

Scope change control involves the recognition that a change has occurred to the project's scope. It is used to carry out the appropriate actions to accommodate the change and to manage the approval or refusal of requests for scope change.

Project managers use schedule control to handle changes that affect the schedule. Schedule control also involves updating the schedule when changes occur in other areas of the project plan.

Cost control involves the realization that project costs have changed from the original estimate. Cost control is used to update the budget and to judge which cost changes require an immediate response.

Quality control is used to make sure the project provides what it promises by measuring and monitoring project deliverables against project requirements.

Risk control is used to assess risks the project faces and to roll out risk prevention strategies and contingency plans across the entire project. Project managers also use risk control to gauge the impact preventive actions have.

If a change is required to be made to any aspect of the project, it is advisable to follow the five-step change control process:

1.   change request submitted
2.   review of the request
3.   accept or reject request
4.   update project baseline and plans, and
5.   communicate change and implement it

Question

Change control can be broken down into five different sections.

What are they?

Options:
1. Scope change control
2. Schedule control

3. Cost control
4. Quality control
5. Risk control
6. Customer relationship control
7. Legislative compliance control

Answer

Option 1: This option is correct. Scope change control is part of change control. It relates to changes made to the scope of the project.
Option 2: This option is correct. Schedule control is a part of change control and involves any changes that affect the project's schedule.
Option 3: This option is correct. Cost control is involved in change control and covers any issues regarding cost differentiation.
Option 4: This option is correct. Quality control is used as part of change control to ensure that the project is delivering according to plan.
Option 5: This option is correct. As part of change control, risk control involves the use of prevention strategies or contingency plans.
Option 6: This option is incorrect. Customer relationship control is not a recognized activity in change control, even though project managers interact with customers for the duration of a project.
Option 7: This option is incorrect. Legislative compliance control is not a separate element of change control.

2. Submitting a change request

The first step in the change control process involves submitting a change request. To initiate this step formally, a change request form is used. This form is an official request from someone connected to the project manager and can either be electronic or paper based. All change requests must be addressed or brought to the attention of the project manager so that he can track and document the request, as well as take action if necessary.

The person submitting the project change request form must describe the change and the reason for it.

The change description should be a brief summary of what the change entails – for example decreasing resources, adding staff, narrowing project scope, and expediting the schedule.

The reason or justification for the change explains why it should occur. Usually, the change is something that brings the project back in line with its goals and with minimal disruption. The reason can also include the client's opinion and a description of how the change will affect deliverables.

The change request form also stipulates the identity of the manager who controls the project and the parties responsible for deciding whether or not the change will be adopted.

If any of the changes exceed the project manager's authority, she will refer them to the change control board, also known as the CCB. The CCB is usually a small group that evaluates the viability of change requests in terms of the request's pertinence and potential impact on the project.

Consider this example of a property surveying company that commissions a project to install a new geographical information system (GIS). One of the project team members believes that the support software they are using is barely adequate for its purpose. He believes that the software will be out of date by the time the project is completed. He fills out a project change request form, describing the change and the justification for it. He submits the form to the project manager.

Question

Which of the following details need to be included in a project change request form?

Options:

1. A description of the change
2. A justification for the change
3. Complete cost breakdown of the change
4. An expert's testimonial to support the change

Answer

Option 1: This option is correct. A description of the change is an essential part of the project change request form. It outlines what the change will entail.

Option 2: This option is correct. A justification for the change must be included in the project change request form. It provides logical reasons for making the request.

Option 3: *This option is incorrect. A complete cost breakdown of the change will be required at a later stage, depending on whether or not the change is approved. At this initial stage, there is no need for such a detailed breakdown.*

Option 4: *This option is incorrect. It is unnecessary to solicit an expert's testimonial to support the change at this initial stage. The project manager or the CCB will assess the strength of the change request.*

3. Reviewing the change request

The second step in the change control process is to review the change request. After the project change request form is submitted, the project manager will record it. Before logging the request, the project manager reads it over to ensure that all the necessary information is included. Once the request is logged, it should be understandable to anyone who needs to reference the file and available to everyone who may need it, such as auditors and project team members.

The project manager, or the CCB if the change exceeds the project manager's authority, then needs to consider the impact of the change in relation to cost, schedule, potential risk, and scope.

It is important to know if there are any existing elements in the project that will clash with the proposed change. It is also necessary to check if there are any earlier changes pending that the current change will clash with.

The risks associated with both making the change and not making the change will then have to be judged.

As project manager, you'll have to decide if implementing the change is within the ability of the project team or whether extra resources will be required.

You'll need to analyze whether implementing the change will affect the sequence or duration of the other tasks in the project plan.

You also need to estimate how much work will be required, in hours, to implement any given change. This is done by calculating the impact on the cost of the project by multiplying the number of estimated hours by the rate.

To calculate the impact on the project's schedule, divide the number of estimated hours into the project's assigned resources. You will then need to summarize the benefits of implementing the change, provided that there are any.

Returning to the example of the property surveying company, after reviewing and logging the request, the project manager assesses the benefits and risks of implementing the change, which involves switching to a newer version of the support software. The change shouldn't affect the schedule too much because the software is available. The team has the ability to use the new software and integrate it with the company's existing operating systems. However, making the change will add to the project's cost.

Question

Match the correct examples of activities in the change control process to the step it describes. Not all activities will match to a step.

Options:

A.   A project team member notices that there is a compatibility problem with an element of an IT project. He completes a form detailing the issue and e-mails it to the project manager.

B.   A project manager logs the project change request form and assesses the benefits and risks associated with it.

C.   A project manager uses a cost performance index to monitor the progress of a task.

Targets:

1. Submitting a change request
2. Reviewing the change request

Answer

This is an example of submitting a change request form, the first step in the change control process. The change is described, justified, and brought to the project manager's attention.

This is an example of reviewing the change request, the second step in the change control process. The request is logged and has its bene-

fits and risks assessed.

4. Accepting or rejecting the request

Accepting or rejecting the request is the third step in the change control process. After assessing the change's potential impact, the project manager or CCB will decide to accept or reject the change.

If the change will be beneficial to the overall project, with little impact on scope, cost, or schedule, or if it will positively impact the project by decreasing costs or moving schedules forward, then the change will typically be accepted.

Should the change be likely to have a negative impact because it requires major scope changes, cost increases, or schedule delays, the change may be rejected.

If a change represents a low-cost addition that will substantially improve the quality of the product, the project manager may choose to execute the change without passing the cost along to the client.

But if the change is critical to the project's success, then the client may have to proceed with the change despite the cost.

During the third step, a formal response to the project change request form is made.

The change impact statement is a summary of the actions that will be required to implement the proposed change.

The statement usually lists the trade-offs the project manager is willing to make to incorporate the change.

There are several different responses a project manager can include in a change impact statement:

- the change is not approved because it doesn't fit in the project's scope
- the change can be made within schedule and with no extra resources required
- the change can be made with the current resources, but the schedule will have to be extended
- the change can be made within the schedule, but extra resources are required

- the change can be made, but the schedule will need to be extended, and extra resources will be required
- the change can be made, but the deliverables will be produced in a tiered strategy, and
- the change cannot be made without extensive changes to the project plan

In the example of the property surveying company, the project manager prepares the change impact statement in relation to upgrading to a new software package.

His response is that the change can be made within the schedule, but extra resources are required. In this case the resources are financial as the new software is very expensive.

Question

True or false? After assessing a change's potential impact, the project manager or CCB will decide to accept or reject the change.

Options:

1. True
2. False

Answer

Correct answer(s):

1. True

5. Documenting and implementing change

Updating the project baseline and plans is the fourth step in the change control process.

Once a request has been accepted and approved, the changes must be documented.

A project manager will often designate this task to a configuration management specialist who will carry out this documentation as well as update the project specifications.

Depending on the size of the project, the configuration management process can be very complex and elaborate. Each change that is documented is assigned a configuration item number and logged.

It is normally the responsibility of the project manager to check that any changes made to project documentation are captured in the correct manner and have received proper approval.

As soon as the change is approved and the files are updated, the change is published. Changes to a project's baseline require a corresponding change to the contract.

The change, requesting that the project for the property surveying company switch to a newer version of the software, is duly documented and assigned a configuration number. The project manager revises the documentation to ensure that the change has been properly recorded.

The final step in the change control process involves communicating the change to the team and implementing it. Communication is a key tool in any process.

IT projects can be hugely complicated with many different parties involved as stakeholders. Some stakeholders may be involved in the change process and so will be aware of the change before others.

But once a change is approved for implementation, it is crucial that all the stakeholders are informed. This ensures that the project's focus is retained and that no one feels slighted at being left out of the loop.

Job Aid

The Change Control Process

Purpose: *Use this job aid to review the five steps in the change control process.*

The five steps in the change control process

STEP 1: SUBMIT A CHANGE REQUEST

A project change request form with a description and justification for the proposed change is submitted to the project manager.

STEP 2: REVIEW THE REQUEST

The project manager (or the CCB if the change exceeds the project manager's authority) considers the impact of the change in relation to cost, schedule, potential risk, and scope.

STEP 3: ACCEPT OR REJECT THE CHANGE

After assessing the change's potential impact, the project manager or CCB will decide to accept or reject the change.

STEP 4: UPDATE THE PROJECT BASELINE AND PLANS

Once a change is accepted, the project baseline and plans must be updated to incorporate this change.

STEP 5: COMMUNICATING THE CHANGE TO THE TEAM AND IMPLEMENTING IT

All stakeholders are informed of the change and its implementation begins.

Finally, the time comes to implement the decision. If the decision is to accept the change, then both the cost and baselines may require adjustments to reflect the impact of the approved change. If the decision affects the scope, cost, or schedule, the project manager adjusts the work breakdown structure, or WBS, and the scope statement to reflect the change. If the decision is to reject the change, the project manager files the documentation and closes the request.

Question

Match the examples of activities in the change control process to the step it describes. Not all scenarios will match a step.

Options:

A.   A project manager on a large ICT infrastructure project assesses the merits of a change

B.   A configuration management specialist documents a series of changes on an IT project involving shared services

C.   The project manager of a LAN upgrade informs all the stakeholders involved of a change to the project

D.   A compatibility issue on a software upgrade project sees a team member completing a project change request form

Targets:

1. Accepting or rejecting the request
2. Updating the project baseline and plans
3. Communicating change and implementing it

Answer

Assessing the merits of a change is part of the decision whether or not to accept a change proposal.

Documenting changes is an example of updating the project baseline and plans.

Keeping stakeholders informed is an example of communicating change and implementing it.

Question

Sequence the activities that occur in the change control process.

Options:

A.   A project manager describes a change she deems necessary and sends a change request form with its description to her manager

B.   The change is reviewed and assessed

C.   It's decided that the change can be made with minor adjustments to the schedule

D.   The change is documented and the schedule and other relevant documents updated

E.   The project manager communicates the change to the team and all the stakeholders in the project

Answer

Correct answer(s):

A project manager describes a change she deems necessary and sends a change request form with its description to her manager is ranked - Submitting a change request form is the first step in the change control process.

The change is reviewed and assessed is ranked - Reviewing the change request is the second step in the change control process. **It's decided that the change can be made with minor adjustments to the schedule is ranked** - Accepting or rejecting the request is the third step in the change control process.

The change is documented and the schedule and other relevant documents updated is ranked - Updating the project baseline and plans is the fourth step in the change control process.

The project manager communicates the change to the team and all the stakeholders in the project is ranked - Communicating the change and implementing it is the fifth step in the change control process.

6. Summary

All projects experience the need for change to some degree despite the best preparation and planning. IT projects are particularly susceptible to change. Project managers use a change control process to manage changes that occur.

The change control process itself involves a five-step approach: submitting a change request form, reviewing the request, accepting or rejecting the request, updating the project baseline and plans, and communicating and implementing the change.

Follow-on Activity

Making Changes to a Project

Purpose: *Use this follow-on activity to review a project you were involved with and consider your answers in light of what you have just learned.*

Consider a change that you deemed valid on a project you worked on in the past.

- Did you incorporate the change into the project plan? If so, why?
- Did any aspect of the change require additional resources, funding, or time?
- What impact did the change have on the project?
- Did you think that the implementation of the change went well? How so?

- Were there areas that could have been improved on, regarding the implementation?

IT PROJECT MANAGEMENT ESSENTIALS: MANAGING RISKS IN AN IT PROJECT

T project managers have to thread a path to success, juggling project goals, resources, and schedules, surrounded by risks on all sides. Every project, no matter how big or small, has risks. Risks are uncertain events that threaten your IT projects due to the effect that uncertainty has on objectives. The pressure to reduce costs and improve project performance, time to market, and management practices is driving organizations to more effectively manage risk to avoid expensive problems.

Knowing how to manage risks can help you effectively manage the project outcome, circumvent unexpected outcomes, and avoid getting bogged down in crisis management. In this course, you'll learn how to identify potential threats to your project's cost, deadlines, or deliverables.

You'll learn about the four common sources of project risk: resource skills and availability, technology requirements and integration, vendors integration and communication, and risks related to project management. These include threats to the scope, schedule, budget, and overall management of the project.

You'll also learn about the three tools for identifying risks: interviews, checklists, and brainstorming. You'll be introduced to risk statements and risk registers, which are effective tools for documentation.

In addition, this course covers how to analyze risk in IT projects, which involves first determining whether or not the risk is within the project scope. If it is, you assess the impact and the probability, and then can prioritize the risks in terms of relative importance. And finally, you'll learn how to use the prioritized list of risks to develop risk response strategies to mitigate or eliminate the impact of the threats to your projects.

Managing Risks in an IT Project
1. Identifying Risks in IT Projects
2. Documenting Risks for an IT Project
3. Analyzing Risks in IT Projects
4. Developing Risk Response Strategies for an IT Project

IDENTIFYING RISKS IN IT PROJECTS

1. Risk identification

When problems arise with an IT project, how many times have you thought to yourself, "If only I'd known that was going to happen?" It would be nice to be able to predict the future, but you don't need a crystal ball. Being able to identify a project's potential risks is the next best thing. Risks are those uncertain events that can cause problems – sometimes severe problems – that threaten the success of IT projects.

Every project, no matter how big or small, has risks. Risks are uncertain or surprise events. They are sometimes threats that can cause a loss of time, quality, money, control, or understanding. The threats may come internally or externally, from shareholders, customers, or even governments or natural disasters.

IT project managers have to try to determine the probable effects of risks and the uncertainties that risks can create. Only then can you put a plan in place to manage the risk on your project.

Risks can occur at any point during a project's development and maintenance. For example, if customer requirements constantly change on a project, there will be a loss of control and understanding among developers, the customer, end users, stakeholders, and the project manager. Everything associated with the project can be affected, from cost to schedule to morale.

Question

All industries experience risk, not just the IT industry. Several categories of risk may be commonly encountered depending on your company or industry. See if you can match each example to its category of risk.

Options:

    A.   Abnormal climatic conditions
    B.   Lack of infrastructure
    C.   Unstable governmental or social environments
    D.   Unauthorized access to confidential information
    E.   Unavailability or unacceptable quality of materials

Targets:

    1. Environmental risk
    2. Operational risk
    3. Geopolitical risk
    4. Information security risk
    5. Supplier risk

Answer

Natural or environmental risks may occur due to abnormal climatic conditions such as flood, earthquake, storms, and drought. Occurrence of these risks can cause heavy damage to an organization's assets.

Operational risk arises due to lack of proper infrastructure and facilities. These risks can lead to loss or damage of operational facilities, services, or equipment.

Geopolitical risks occur due to unstable political and social environments in countries. These risks can also arise due to cultural differences or a lack of quality infrastructure in a country.

Information security risk occurs when unauthorized people access and use confidential information.

Supplier risk arises when the organization does not conduct proper evaluation of the suppliers' capabilities. These risks include aspects such as supply of low-quality materials, improper maintenance of supply chain, and unavailability of materials.

No matter what industry you're in, risk events are always likely to affect projects significantly. Project managers have to be able to identify all potential risks before they can isolate causes and determine impacts. Identifying risks helps you determine the probability of the risk occurring and its consequences.

Project risk is about not achieving your objectives within time, cost, and resource parameters. It includes all possibilities of suffering loss during a project life cycle. Losses influence the project in the form of lower-end product quality, increased costs, delayed completion, or project failure.

Keep in mind that risk is a threat that may never materialize. So the outcome of a risk event is the important part, since that's what can impact the project. Impacts affect a project's scope, schedule, budget, and stakeholder satisfaction.

Although most people think of risk as a bad thing, it's actually two-sided. With any risk there's an opportunity for gain as well as loss. For example, suppose a customer for a web site project wants another level of functionality added. This change to the project scope might be negative for the web developer if there isn't enough time or expertise available. But on the other hand, the change could produce more revenue if the developer can manage the risk.

In the case of scope change, the web developer might be able to manage the risk by hiring skilled resources, working with another company that has the expertise, or subcontracting or outsourcing that component of the work.

Risks in IT projects tend to be extreme. Losses can be significant, but gains can also be immense if the risk is planned for and well managed.

The key is being able to recognize the risks and determine if they can be directed and controlled. If risk can't be managed to produce a neutral or positive impact on a project, then perhaps the project shouldn't be attempted.

So how can you tell if risks can only be negative? You need to look at the three components of risk: the event itself, the probability that the event will happen, and the impact on the project if the event occurs. For example, John is managing a project to update his company's system software. One of his experienced coders may be needed on another project.

Event

John identifies a risk event as something that can happen to the project, whether good or bad. In his situation, a delay in deliverables might occur if he loses an experienced coder.

Probability

The probability of a risk such as a missed deadline occurring are the chances the event will happen. John asks himself, "What are the odds that losing this coder will cause a delay?"

Impact

John also looks at the impact losing the coder might have on the project. He analyzes the potential effects on the project, good or bad, if the event occurs by asking himself "How severely will this affect the project?" and "What is the worst possible loss associated with this?"

It's easy to confuse risks with the everyday problems or issues you deal with all the time. Risks are events that may or may not occur in the future, while issues occur in the present and have to be managed immediately.

Consider this situation. A localization project for a software company is dependent on a new translation tool. There's a 30% chance that the delivery of the tool will be late, causing a delay in the schedule. This is a risk the company must identify. It could happen in the future, but once it's identified, it can be planned for.

An issue, on the other hand, would be if the shipping company that was delivering the tool lost the package. This is an immediate problem that has to be addressed right away.

Projects, by their very nature, are more vulnerable to risks and issues than daily processes and operations. Projects are one-time activities that aren't ongoing or repetitive, so known hazards and solutions don't always apply. But if you develop defined and proven risk management techniques, you can mitigate the effects of common project risks such as budget cuts, unclear or unspecific project goals, unrealistic schedules, and quality issues.

The importance of early risk identification

It's crucial that risks be identified early on in project planning so adequate systems can be put in place to effectively manage those risks throughout the life of the project. Managers and executives know about big-picture risks, but line workers and team members can also have vital information about project-level hazards. Risk management consists of processes, methods, and tools for managing all the threats to IT projects before they turn into real problems.

2. Sources of risk

Before risks can be managed, you need to find their sources. These sources may be internal or external, ranging from project stakeholders and employees to the weather. There are four main sources of risk associated with IT projects: team members, technology, vendors, and project management.

Risks arising from team members usually relate to their skills and availability.

Whether due to an initial lack of funds, people joining the team late, or members leaving, team member risk can result in the project team having insufficient skills on board to complete the project.

The schedule can be impacted by the reassignment of staff to other projects, a lack of required resources, or unrealistic expectations for staff members. These risks can result in missed deadlines.

Technology risks can lead to unsatisfactory or failed product functions. Examples of these risks can include problems resulting from the use of outdated or inappropriate technology, software that doesn't work as planned, or integration difficulties. Technology risks are usually related to either requirements or testing.

Requirement risks

Equipment requirement risks can range from necessary hardware not being delivered on time, to access to a development environment being restricted. And of course, equipment can always fail or have technical or performance limitations that put the project at risk.

Testing risks

During the testing of an IT project – which is usually undertaken at the end of the process – an installation or upgrade might be found to be unstable, quality might be substandard, software might be unsuited to the set task, or the user interface might be too complex to use without training.

The third area of risk type in IT projects is related to vendors. Vendor risk includes having to integrate deliverables into in-house processes, and the communication and geopolitical risks of developing parts of projects offshore.

The use of untested subcontractors may contribute to un-certainty. Planned or unplanned changes to the contracts of vendors committed to the project may also generate negative risks.

With vendors, there's always the possibility that the subcontractors will under-perform. They may fail to meet deadlines, their response time may not be adequate, or your project's requirements may exceed their available capacity. Outsourcing is often a primary cause of project delay, since even when deliverable inspection is undertaken, it's often too late in the process to mitigate risk.

The final area of risk types in IT projects is related to the management of the project itself. Project managers need to take the time to work with the project team and other stakeholders to formally determine and document where their particular project is at risk. These risk areas typically include threats to scope, schedule, budget, and management.

Scope

Risks to scope and project requirements include uncontrolled change requests and bad scope definition. If a project is unable to meet a client's desired goal or attain unfamiliar objectives, scope creep will be generated, which is when the scope of a project inflates over time.

Schedule

Schedule risks may arise if initial estimates are too aggressive or otherwise inaccurate. Projects may also fall behind schedule because decisions are not made efficiently.

Budget

Managerial or administrative failures may cause the budget to suffer if it becomes difficult to get the funding you need to complete tasks. Cost risks can also include cost overruns by other members of the team, unmanaged changes, or inaccurate cost estimations.

Management

Management risks to the project's viability can occur whenever a project is inefficiently managed or a manager is inexperienced. Change requests are a significant source of management difficulty, especially if the requests are made by people who weren't involved in the requirement identification process. Management risks also include poor personnel management, such as over-committing team members or not staffing projects appropriately.

Question

You're an IT project manager at a health care company. You're beginning a large, long-term project to computerize the mostly manual and paper-based operation. Match common sources of risk in an IT project to examples from this project.

Options:

    A.   Team members
    B.   Technology
    C.   Vendors
    D.   Project management

Targets:

1. Some of your data entry workers may soon leave or be transferred
2. The new database has to be integrated into your existing system
3. The part of the project that is being outsourced may

not meet your standards

4. The simple database that was originally planned may need to be expanded

Answer

Team member availability is a source of risk in an IT project, especially considering employee attrition over a long period of time.

Technology is a source of risk in an IT project. The technology itself, such as a new database, may be difficult to merge with your existing technology.

Vendors are a source of risk in an IT project, because subcontractors don't always meet quality or schedule requirements.

Project management is a source of risk in an IT project. If change isn't managed well, the scope of the project may increase.

3. Tools to identify risk

Risks aren't just the external threats that can negatively affect projects. Risks also comprise how well your resources and capabilities match your project's needs. At this point, you might be wondering if you can ever identify all the possible risks to your projects. Using tools to identify the strengths, weaknesses, opportunities, and threats facing your project can help you avoid unknown issues by planning for success. Three common tools used in risk identification are interviews, checklists, and brainstorming.

Interviews

Interviewing team members helps you identify risk. The people who know the most about project risks are the people who work on the project, so you should interview them one-on-one or have a team meeting dedicated to identifying these risks. During the interviews, make sure you explore each person's area of expertise. For example, you could review the technical documentation with the technical team lead and discuss resource allocation with the person in charge of the project's budget.

When you interview project stakeholders, consider asking them what they would be worried about if they were managing your project. You can often discover overlooked risk areas with such a question.

Checklists

Checklists are a way to list all the potential risks you discover. You can develop checklists from historical data you collect, lessons learned, or from stakeholder interviews. Your team can review previously completed projects to identify any risks that might occur in your current IT project.

Checklists help you evaluate project risk by organizing data and questions about threats and uncertainties. However, checklists are never comprehensive so it's best to use another risk identification tool as well. If your company undertakes similar projects regularly, you might want to develop a risk identification checklist or template to help you identify the typical risks associated with the projects in your organization.

Brainstorming

Brainstorming can expedite the risk identification process. You can use a questionnaire or a cause-and-effect diagram, such as a flowchart, to help facilitate brainstorming sessions.

In a brainstorming session, you gather together everyone who can give you input on the project's risks, from the team and technical experts to the customer and project sponsor. Then the team starts generating ideas, without judging or prioritizing them. Once you have a comprehensive list of risks, you can narrow them down by identifying how likely they are and what impact they might have.

Question
Match the tools you can use to help identify risks in an IT project to their descriptions.

Options:
    A.   Interviews
    B.   Checklists
    C.   Brainstorming

Targets:

1. One-on-one or team meetings dedicated to identifying project risks
2. A method of organizing historical data, lessons learned, and stakeholder interviews
3. Generating a list of risks without judging or prioritizing the ideas

Answer

Having either one-on-one or team meetings is a description of interviewing people. By asking the experts who are doing the project work, you'll be able to find out what risks they feel are likely.

Checklists help you organize data and information so you can easily tell if you've covered all risk areas.

When you hold a brainstorming session, you generate a large list of ideas without initially evaluating them. This helps you ensure you've covered all risk areas.

4. Summary

As a project manager, you need to plan for the unexpected. Before you can manage risks in your project, you have to be able to identify them. In IT projects, there are commonly four sources of risk. Team members may not have the skills you need or availability. The technology may not be what the project needs, may not be tested, or may be difficult to integrate into your current systems. Vendors may also pose an integration risk, as well as geopolitical and communication risks if part of the project is developed offshore. And finally, project management-related risks include threats to the scope, schedule, budget, and overall management of the project.

Project risks can be found throughout a project's life cycle. To identify potential risks, you should think of events that could cause risks, and which areas of the project may be affected by each event. You can use three tools for identifying risks: interviews, checklists, and brainstorming.

Follow-on Activity
Risk Identification

Purpose: *Use this follow-on activity to help you identify risks on your IT projects.*

What kinds of risks have you encountered on previous or current IT projects? Categorize them into the following groups:

- Team members
- Technology
- Vendors
- Project management

Now examine the risks to determine if there's any one source group that is more common than others. If so, why do you think that is the case?

Now think about tools you can use to identify risks – interviews, checklists, and brainstorming. Have any of these been effective for you in identifying risks? How so?

DOCUMENTING RISKS FOR AN IT PROJECT

1. Creating risk statements and registers

Once you've identified the risks to your project, you need to document them in a structured way. Only then will you be able to describe and communicate the risks to management. You can do this by creating risk statements and a risk register. **Risk statements** outline the risk, its probability of occurrence, and the areas it will impact. **Risk registers** are spreadsheets or databases of information about all the risks, and include details on the actions needed to mitigate them.

There are three general guidelines for creating clear and descriptive risk statements:

- be as specific as possible when describing the risk event
- explain the impact and state the cause of the risk, and
- don't include any possible responses to the risk or any ideas on how to mitigate it

Be specific

Make your risk statements as specific as you possibly can. A vague statement such as "the first milestone might be delayed" only communicates the effect of the risk – the delay. Such a statement doesn't describe the cause, so it won't help you manage it.

Explain impact and cause

Risk statements need to give clear and useful information about the risk event and the possible impact on the project. For example, instead of simply saying "The manufacturer has informed us that the shipment of chips could be late," the risk statement should say "The shipment of chips could be late due to a backlog at the manufacturer's production facility, which would in turn cause a delay in the creation of our prototype."

Don't include risk responses

Solutions, mitigating actions, and responses to the risks should not be in the risk statement. In the initial stages of risk identification and documentation, you may not know the probability or the true extent of the impact. Right now, you're just stating the risk events, the cause, and what you know of the impact. Later in the risk management process, you'll have more information as you analyze the identified risks.

You can use a kind of template to create risk statements by simply filling in the relevant information in this sentence: "As a result of this cause, that event may happen, which would lead to this impact." For example, you could use the template to rewrite a vague statement such as "the first milestone might be delayed" and change it to "Because of personnel shortages, the first milestone might be delayed, which would delay the vendor handoff."

Question

Consider this risk statement: "Most of the graphic media needs to be created with Flash Animation; the time required to train the graphics team in Flash will extend the project's schedule by two months."

Does this risk statement illustrate all three guidelines?

Options:

1. Yes
2. No

Answer

The statement illustrates the guidelines, specifically stating the potential impact – a two-month delay – and the cause of the risk, which is the need for training. The statement appropriately avoids mentioning possible responses.

A **risk register** documents all of the identified risks related to a particular project or process. It contains the information from the risk statement – the specific description of cause and impact. A risk register entry also identifies the probability of occurrence, a list of the mitigating actions taken to reduce the likelihood or potential impact, and the planned response should the event occur.

The risk register is a living document that records the characteristics of all the risks, as well as subsequent actions and results. As such, it's a vital tool for monitoring and controlling risk and for evaluating the effects of various actions. Project managers can use it to examine the overall risk status at any point in time.

Risk registers may be expanded to include other information that's valuable to risk management, such as symptoms, warning signs, response personnel, and secondary risks. Risks usually have priority rankings assigned for easy identification.

Question

Which risk statement would be the most effective for an IT software application project?

Options:

1. "If the use of smartphones continues to increase, our application software will need to be rewritten for them, which will delay development by three weeks."

2. "If the use of smartphones continues to increase, the basic software will need to be rewritten to accommodate their use. This will delay development by three weeks. This is our highest ranking risk, with a probability of 45%."

3. "Some of our software may need to be rewritten if popular trends change. Several different versions will be produced to ensure this isn't a major problem."

Answer

Option 1: *This is the correct option. This risk statement follows the guidelines by being specific about cause – the increase in smartphone use – and potential impact on the schedule.*

Option 2: *This is an incorrect option. Although this statement in-*

cludes a specific description of the risk, its potential impact, and its cause, it also includes information about rank and probability, which is more suited to the risk register.

Option 3: *This is an incorrect option. This risk statement doesn't follow the guidelines. It's not specific, as it doesn't answer questions such as "Which software?" and "How much will need to be rewritten?" and "Which changing trends will trigger this impact?"*

2. Summary

Risk statements describe a risk specifically, detailing its cause and potential impact. They do not include potential solutions or mitigating actions.

The risk register is the final output of the risk identification process, and is a key tool in risk management because it captures all of the information relating to project risks. It provides a clear view of the status of each risk and the status of overall project risk at any given point in time.

ANALYZING RISKS IN IT PROJECTS

1. Benefits of risk analysis

Almost everything in the business world involves a risk. After all, your customers' habits change constantly, new competitors arise in your market, and factors outside of your control can impact your project's schedule. IT project managers have to try to determine the probable effects of these kinds of threats and the uncertainties that they can create, so managers must devise a process or plan to analyze the risk on projects.

After you've identified all the risks in your project, you may be intimidated by the sheer number of things that could go wrong. You may even think the project can never succeed.

But keep in mind that these are just potential threats – things that might happen, but that might not. And these threats might also bring opportunities, if they are handled correctly.

The only way to gauge their true impact is to analyze the risks after they've been identified. When you quantify the potential threats, you can focus on the ones with the greatest impact on your project.

Analyzing risks is a vital step in managing them. As an IT project manager, you probably deal with potential problems every day. But if you don't have a risk management plan or process in place, you're probably managing reactively instead of proactively. Reactive management means your team could go over budget, miss deadlines, or even impact the firm's reputation. Having an IT project risk management process will help you monitor these threats during the entire life of your IT project.

You will encounter project-specific risks for each of your IT projects. You will also have similar threats from project to project. Risk analysis can help you with the specific issues for any size project. Analyzing project risks can benefit you in several ways:

- You can develop effective strategies and plans to manage project risks. This can shorten the response time in a crisis and limit or even reverse damage caused if the problem does occur.
- You decrease the possibility of risks having adverse effects on the project's goals and increase the chances of positive risks that are opportunities. This leads to fewer bad impacts and more good ones.

Formal risk analysis and management help you assess potential threats and decide what actions to take to minimize disruptions to your project. They also help you determine if risk control strategies will be cost effective.

Being able to deal with uncertain project events in such a proactive manner allows you to minimize the impact of threats and seize any opportunities that occur. You'll be better able to deliver your project on time, within budget, and to the quality standards required.

Question

If Stephan, an IT project manager, were asked how he could benefit from using project risk analysis, what do you think he might say?

Options:

1. "I will be able to develop effective strategies and plans to manage risks that could negatively affect the success of my IT projects."
2. "I will be able to decrease the chance of risks adversely impacting my project's objectives, and increase the likelihood of positive risks that aid the project."
3. "I will be able to effectively construct a plan that will get me a promotion."
4. "I'll be able to identify the needs that arise from the organization as a whole."

Answer

Option 1: This is a correct option. When you can analyze risks, you can develop the strategies you need to manage them. And effective strategies can control the damage a risk can cause if it happens.

Option 2: This is a correct option. Through analyzing risks, you can decrease the possibility of adverse effects and increase the chance of opportunities occurring.

Option 3: This is an incorrect option. Analyzing project risks may contribute to the success of your project, but will not guarantee you a promotion.

Option 4: This is an incorrect option. Analyzing your own project's risks will help you manage them, but won't help you with a needs analysis.

2. The risk analysis process

Risk analysis is a structured way to first recognize and then concentrate on the threats that are the most significant to your project. Using it, you can assess the risks and uncertainties that might threaten your project. The outputs of this analysis are categorized and prioritized risks and the identification of the most important contributors to project uncertainty. There are two main approaches: qualitative and quantitative.

Qualitative risk analysis

Qualitative analysis uses a relative measure based on separating risks into descriptive categories such as low, medium, or high. Because qualitative analysis helps you determine the impact of the risks on the project as well as their likelihood of occurrence, you can prioritize them according to their effect.

This type of analysis is a simplified approach that you can do without special tools or training. Because it analyzes probability and impact, you can focus on the risks that really need attention.

Quantitative risk analysis

Quantitative analysis gives numerical results that express percentages, values, and probabilities. This method is a complex and mathematical approach that allows you to numerically analyze the risks. The outputs of quantitative analysis are numeric probabilities of occurrence, the effect on the project goals, and any overall consequences.

The tools available for computing quantitative risk analysis include statistical simulation using the Monte Carlo technique, sensitivity analysis, decision tree analysis, and interviewing. These tools are typically used by risk analysis experts to complete a threat assessment or to help project teams.

In this topic, the focus is on a simplified approach to qualitative risk analysis. Since not all risks are equal, IT project managers need to be able to focus on the ones with the greatest potential impact on the project's success.

Although all threats should be included in a risk analysis, special attention must be given to those at the high-risk end of the list. After all, some risks can be more threatening to the success of your project than others.

While they don't all have to be followed in a sequential order, there are four main phases in the risk-analysis process:

- determine whether the risk is within the project scope
- assess the impact of the risk on the project's objectives
- assess the probability of the risk occurring, and
- prioritize the risks to determine the importance they can have on your project

3. Determining if the risk is in scope

Each of the risks you've identified first needs to be assessed to determine whether or not it's within the existing scope of the project. The project scope describes all the work required to create the product or deliverable, and only the required work. When analyzing the risks, you determine if the action generating the perceived risk is within the scope of the work. If not, it's probably not a threat to the project and can be ignored.

To determine if the risk is in scope, consider whether the event would impact the fit, form, or function of the project deliverables. When you brainstormed to identify all risks, you might have generated a potential threat that may turn out not to be a problem after all. Or, if it is still a risk, the consequences of the impact might be so small that they don't have to be a concern.

For example, suppose an eBusiness team has a development project to design and build a web site for a manufacturing company. The site needs to detail all the company's products and provide links to online retailers where the products can be purchased.

The team came up with a list of risks that included having to deal with constantly changing product prices. However, this was a perceived problem that isn't actually a threat when you measure it against the project scope. Since external vendors will be selling the products, price updates will be their responsibility, not the development team's.

Question

In the same eBusiness web site development example, another risk the team identified was having to spend more time developing the site to enable additional products to be easily added to it over a period of time.

Do you think this risk is within the scope of this project?

Options:

1. Yes
2. No

Answer

In this case, the action generating the perceived risk is within the scope of the project. The project is to showcase all the manufacturer's products, so making the product list updatable will be something your team needs to deal with. It is a risk that can't be ignored.

4. Assessing the risk impact

After deciding that a risk is within scope, the next phase in risk analysis is to determine the impact to the project if the event occurs. For each of the threats you identified, you have to assess the effect on the project if the problem happens.

A risk always has an impact if it occurs; otherwise, it wouldn't be classified as a risk at all. But how big the impact will be in terms of cost, schedule, quality, or customer satisfaction will vary.

In qualitative risk analysis, you assess impact using a simple rating system such as high impact, medium impact, or low impact. On a medium or large project, you may want to establish some guidelines that indicate what each ranking means against these categories. In general, high impact means there's a significant effect on a project's objectives. Medium means some impact on individual project deliverables but minimal damage to the overall project, and low indicates minimal impact to any project deliverable.

It helps to look at impacts in different areas. Be sure to draw on the judgment of team members and any historical data you have when assessing impact, because each team member will have valuable expert knowledge of different subjects. While most risks you deal with will affect many or all of the areas, the main impact will be in one region. Areas common to most IT projects are schedule risk, scope-performance-quality or SPQ risk, budget risk, and stakeholder satisfaction risk.

Select each area for examples of impacts on IT projects.

Schedule risk

The most common schedule risk in IT projects is when deadlines slip and schedule overruns occur.

Impacts can range from low to high in this area, depending on how much longer a project may take to complete than has been estimated, and in what stage of the project's life cycle the overrun occurs.

SPQ risk

The scope-performance-quality or SPQ risks include examples such as process changes that lead to increased work and time needed, or when a new application or system isn't fully compatible with the existing infrastructure.

Scope-related risks account for a large proportion of most project's cumulative schedule delays.

Budget risk

Budget risks often occur in conjunction with schedule risks and SPQ risks. The impact of fixing problems or getting back on track almost always ends up with projects costing more than initially expected.

Impacts can range from low, when costs are close to the projected values, to high, if budgets have to be almost doubled.

Stakeholder satisfaction risk

You might recognize stakeholder satisfaction risk if end users are unable or unwilling to use a new system or don't obtain all of the benefits they expect.

Anytime there is technical performance that doesn't meet stakeholder expectations, their satisfaction will be impacted.

For example, a fitness company needs a mobile phone version of its web site. The site is complex, allowing users to update individual food, exercise, and health logs. The team developing the application identifies three risks associated with the project: running out of money before completion, losing personnel to higher priority projects, and needing to rewrite the documentation due to changes to standards. The budget risk is high impact, the resource risk is medium impact, and the rework is low impact.

5. Assessing risk probability

The third phase in analyzing project risk is to assess the probability of each event. Risk probability occurrence ranges from a little over 0% to a little under 100%. If there was a 100% probability, the risk would be a certainty, not a potential threat. And at exactly 0%, there's no potential at all. As with impact assessment, you can use high, medium, and low rankings, but you should establish guidelines as to what those ratings mean.

Analyzing a risk's probability is usually a bit subjective, since it's an assessment of the chances of something happening based on experience and level of comfort.

For example, a conservative company might set its guidelines for high probability at 40%, and low probability at 10% or less. Another organization might set high at a likelihood of 60% or greater, medium at 20 to 60%, and low at less than 20%.

Question

The fitness company developing a mobile phone version of their website has set guidelines for risk probability. Low probability is considered to be under 15%, medium is 16-50%, and high is over 50%. Of the three main risks associated with the project, running out of money before completion has a 55% chance of occurring, losing personnel to higher priority projects has a 75% chance, and needing to rewrite the documentation due to changes to standards has a 20% likelihood.

Match each risk to its probability assessment category. The categories may have more than one match, and some categories may not be used.

Options:

A.   Budget risk
B.   Resource risk
C.   Rework risk

Targets:

1. High
2. Medium
3. Low

Answer

Since the company defines high risk as anything above 50%, the budget risk – at 55% – and the resource risk – at 75% – are both high probability.

The company defines medium risk as between 16% and 50%, so the rework risk, at 20%, falls into the medium probability category.

None of the identified risks have a probability of less than 15%.

For a medium or large project, it may be appropriate to be more sophisticated and establish risk rankings of 1 to 5 or 1 to 10. Guidelines should be put in place to establish what the rankings mean, such as assigning 1 to a very low risk with probability of less than 5%, 2 to a low risk of between 6 and 15%, and so forth. Whenever possible, try to assign a percentage probability to the risk, which will be helpful when you prioritize the risks in the next step.

6. Prioritizing risks

The final phase in risk analysis is prioritization. In some ways, it would be nice to treat all the risks equally. It would certainly make work simpler. But it wouldn't give you the best results, because some threats have a higher impact or greater chance of occurring. You need to spend your time on the risks causing the biggest losses and gains. Trying to address each and every problem your project might face is usually too expensive in time and resources.

You can't manage all the risks you've identified. In most cases, you can only manage about ten at a time. Your top ten should be actively managed, and a watch list kept of the remaining threats. Those remainders can move onto the active management list as replacements for any risks that are mitigated, controlled, eliminated, or don't occur. Of course, in some businesses – such as in the airline industry – you need to pay attention to even very unlikely risks. Where a potential threat involves injury or loss of life, all need to be managed.

Once you have determined the severity of impact and probability of occurrence, you can prioritize the risks logically. A risk prioritization matrix is useful for a visual representation of the importance of each project risk.

Using the matrix, the project manager assesses the probability and impact of each risk and plots it on the chart. The probability that a risk will occur is represented on one axis, and the impact of the risk, if it were to happen, on the other.

This matrix provides a useful framework to help you determine which risks need your attention the most. You end up with a clear view of the priority to give to each risk, since risks are ranked from high probability and high impact to low probability and low impact.

Using the matrix, each risk's position determines its priority. Select each quadrant of the matrix for more information.

High probability, high impact

Risks in the top right corner are of critical importance. With both high impact and high probability, they should be your top priorities.

High impact, low probability

Risks in the top left corner are high impact but low probability. While they're not likely to happen, they are of high importance if they do occur. You should have contingency plans for these risks, in case they happen.

Low impact, high probability

In the bottom right corner are low impact but high probability risks. These are of moderate importance, because while they are likely to happen, you'll be able to deal with them and move on.

Low impact, low probability

In the bottom left corner are low impact and low probability risks. You may be able to ignore these low level risks.

In the fitness company mobile phone website example, the budget risk and the resource risk are high probability, while the rework risk is medium probability. In terms of severity, the budget risk is high impact, the resource risk is medium impact, and the rework is low impact. After plotting the threats on the matrix, it's clear that the budget risk is of critical importance.

Question

You're an IT project manager on a major systems updating project. You've identified a list of risks, including potential schedule and quality problems.

What steps can you take to analyze these risks?

Options:

1. Determine that the schedule risk has a high impact and the quality risks a low impact
2. Determine that the schedule risk has a high probability and the quality risk a low probability

3. Prioritize the risks so the schedule risk has highest importance
4. Determine that both risks are within the scope of what the project has to deliver
5. Compare the ratio of impact to probability for each risk
6. Determine that the schedule risk is likely to happen and ask for more time to complete the project

Answer

Option 1: This is a correct option. Assessing the risk impact by rating them into groupings is an important step in risk analysis. In qualitative risk analysis, you assess impact using a simple rating system such as high impact, medium impact, or low impact.

Option 2: This is a correct option. Assessing the risk probability or chance of occurrence is an integral part to being able to prioritize it. As with impact assessment, you can use high, medium, and low rankings.

Option 3: This is a correct option. The final step in risks analysis is to prioritize using the criteria of impact and probability.

Option 4: This is a correct option. The first step in risk analysis is to figure out if risks are within the project scope. If not, they won't be a threat to the project.

Option 5: This is an incorrect option. When prioritizing risks, you use the combined information in a matrix, you don't use ratios.

Option 6: This is an incorrect option. In the risk analysis stage, you're assessing and prioritizing, not managing or controlling them.

7. Summary

As not all risks become a reality, you have to have a plan to analyze those you identify. Analyzing risks helps you develop effective strategies and plans to manage them. It helps you decrease the possibility they will have adverse effects on the project's objectives and increase the likelihood of positive effects.

To analyze project risks effectively, you first determine whether the risks are within the project scope, then assess both the impact and the probability. Once you know the severity and likelihood of occurrence, you can prioritize the risks in terms of relative importance.

Job Aid

Risk Analysis

Purpose: *Use this job aid as a reference to help you analyze risks on IT projects.*

A table summarizing the steps used to analyze identified risks	
Action	**Techniques**
Determine whether the risk is within the project scope	• Consider whether the risk event will impact fit, form, or function of the project deliverables • If the action generating the perceived risk is not within the scope, it is not a risk and can be ignored
Assess the impact of the risk on the project's objectives	• Identify the impact to the project if the potential problem does occur • Use a simple rating such as high impact, medium impact, and low impact, but set guidelines that indicate what each ranking means • Examine impact in different areas: schedule risk, scope/performance/quality risk, budget risk, and stakeholder satisfaction
Assess the probability of the risk	• Rate the probability of risk occurrence

occurring	· Use ratings of high, medium, and low, but establish guidelines around what these ratings mean · For a medium or large project, establish risk rankings of 1-5 or 1-10
Prioritize the risks to determine the importance they can have on your project	· After you have determined severity and probability, you can prioritize the risks · Use a risk prioritization matrix to plot the risks along axes of impact and probability

DEVELOPING RISK RESPONSE STRATEGIES FOR AN IT PROJECT

1. Transferring risk

After you've identified risks, documented them, and analyzed them, what's next? In risk response planning, you review each item on the prioritized list and determine what action to take. A brainstorming session with the team can help you explore possible responses. The list of potential risk response strategies doesn't have to be comprehensive or exhaustive. It can simply be suggestions to help address threats that would otherwise have a negative impact on the project's success.

When you have risk response strategies in mind, you take a pro-active approach to managing the events. After all, identifying and analyzing risk will only take you so far. You still have to figure out how to respond in case the threat occurs.

Some business risks are predictable and under your control, and others are not. Risk management is particularly vital because some losses – for instance, scope increase, integration problems, or even fires or floods – can affect day-to-day operations and reduce profits. In some cases, events can cause financial hardship severe enough to cripple or even bankrupt a business.

Some risks are positive and can be considered opportunities. The responses to positive risks are to exploit the opportunity, share it with someone who can take better advantage of it, find ways to increase its probability and impact, or to just accept it.

The responses to negative risks need to be more nuanced. There are four response strategies when planning for negative risk:

- transference, where you move the liability for the risk to a third party
- avoidance, in which you change the project plan to eliminate the activity that created the risk
- mitigation, which involves finding strategies to reduce the risk's probability, impact, or both, and
- acceptance, in which you resign yourself to the consequences of the risk or of being unable to transfer, avoid, or mitigate the risk

The first risk response strategy is transference. This technique involves tools such as insurance, performance bonds, or fixed-price contracts to limit or transfer financial risk. When using transference, the third party has to be capable of reducing the threat's probability and, ideally, impact. Secondary risks in transference range from the financial risk of insurance premiums or the schedule risk of an external vendor delivering late. Contracts and insurance are the most common tools for transferring risk.

Insurance

Insurance allows you to transfer risks by exchanging a premium payment for protection against accidents, theft, destruction of property, employee injuries, and many other risks. When you can't provide enough protection using other risk management options, the insurance option is usually chosen.

For instance, consider a web content development company that works with a lot of global contractors. That firm could purchase insurance to help transfer any losses due to intellectual property theft.

Contracts

Contracts help transfer risks by transferring the responsibility for managing the risk event. In practice, this usually occurs when a project needs expertise a company doesn't have. By teaming up with another firm or by hiring a consultant or vendor, you transfer the performance risk.

However, there is still secondary risk involved. You may transfer, via a contract, the risk of meeting your project's deadlines. But if the vendor delivers late, your project will still be late. Not all of the risk will be transferred, although contracts can reduce the probability of the risk happening, and the impact if it does happen.

2. Preventing risk

The next two risk response strategies involve preventing problems from occurring. When you review the prioritized list of risks, you may find that you can take steps to prevent or reduce the chances of the threat happening. Preventive action includes the strategies of avoidance and mitigation.

Risks occur in every project. In fact, you wouldn't want to structure a project to have no risks, because you'd also have no opportunity. But you can use avoidance to consider alternatives with less chance for losses. When you avoid risk, you make a change to the project or the product to reduce or eliminate a threat. You should always try to avoid risks with high impact and high or medium probability.

Consider this situation. Juan, an IT project manager for a software development company, is in charge of a project to build a new financial application for a customer. Juan's lead graphics engineer has identified a high impact, medium probability risk.

The risk statement reads "The graphics integration phase may not finish on time because we are unfamiliar with the customer's proprietary graphics library." To avoid this threat entirely, Juan might have the option of using his own department's current graphics database.

The risk would be eliminated because the graphics department is already familiar with this library. You can use familiar and stable technology, rather than new or untested technology, to avoid risks.

But it's not always possible to eliminate risk entirely. In those cases, you need to mitigate the threat by reducing the probability the event will occur, reducing its impact if it does happen, or both. For instance, in Juan's situation with a potential integration delay, he may not be able to use his department's graphics library – the customer may have specified using theirs. So what can Juan do to reduce the chance or impact of a project delay?

Mitigation usually occurs when you add resources, use better-trained or more experienced personnel, or adopt a best-practice approach. Juan could take a variety of approaches. He could send people for training on the new database, or he could build in more time for the graphics part of the process.

In Juan's case, just sending people for training might mitigate a high probability, medium impact risk down to a more acceptable level of low probability and medium impact.

The level of impact – that is, increases in cost or schedule – may not be reduced, but the chances of the risk event happening would be much smaller.

Question

Your company is developing a software system to run on flash memory. A new version of the flash memory is developed just before your system is completed.

If you continue using the previous version until the end of the project, what risk response strategy have you used?

Options:

1. Transference
2. Avoidance
3. Mitigation
4. Acceptance

Answer

Option 1: *This is an incorrect option. In transference, you transfer the risk to a third party, which is not the case in this scenario.*

Option 2: *This is the correct option. New versions of technology may* have defects, so you avoid those potential risks if you keep using the old version. When you use familiar and tested technology, instead of new technology, you avoid risk.

Option 3: This is an incorrect option. Mitigation involves reducing the impact or the probability of the event occurring, or both. In this case, the probability isn't mitigated, it's avoided altogether.

Option 4: This is an incorrect option. Accepting the risk involved with using the new version would arise if you actually used the new version instead of staying with the old one.

With both of the preventive action strategies, avoidance and mitigation, you have to judge the cost of the actions against the impact of the risk. As you identify preventive actions, consider several areas:

- the root causes of the risk, and if you can address one root cause and eliminate or reduce a series of risks
- if the preventive actions are cost-effective, or if they aren't economical in terms of benefits produced by the money that is spent, and
- If there are resources available with the skill set to implement the preventive action

3. Accepting risk

Risk mitigation is a form of acceptance. But in mitigation, you make an attempt to reduce the event's impact or probability. Sometimes, though, you might accept risk with no mitigating actions. You expect the uncertainty and decide it's tolerable as is. If a risk is low impact and low probability, mitigating it may be more trouble than just handling it if it happens. Or you may mitigate a threat as much as you can, then choose to accept any residual risk.

When the risk is known, and the level of impact to the project is within the tolerance level of the project team or organization, acceptance is an option. Often, this kind of threat results from resource unpredictability or availability. There's always a level of risk when you have to share personnel across projects, as schedules can be impacted if resources aren't on hand when they're needed. Usually, though, such a risk is low impact, as other resources can be shifted.

But what happens if you have a risk with a high chance of happening, a high impact, and you've unsuccessfully tried to find ways of reducing the likelihood of the event? If you can't reduce the threat to an acceptable level, if mitigation has resulted in residual risk that's still too great, or if the problem is outside the control of the project team, you need a contingency plan.

A contingency plan describes what you'll do to reduce the impact if an event occurs. The plan should lay out what the most likely impacts to the project would be if the problem occurs, and what can be done to minimize the impacts.

For instance, there are risks you can't prevent, such as strikes or pending legislation. A contingency plan might include working overtime, subcontracting, moving to a new area, or anything to help reduce a risk's impact.

But no matter how good your plans are, you still need to have a clear picture of what's going on with your project. You need to keep track of the identified risks, monitor the effectiveness of your responses, and identify new or changed threats.

A good response plan includes risk triggers. Just as hearing thunder signals that a storm is on the way, triggers alert the project team of impending risk events. Tracking risk response entails monitoring both triggers and the effectiveness of the planned response strategy. Then you can determine if an alternative approach is needed.

Of course, you also need to identify new threats that may occur as a result of implementing your response strategies. Project assumptions may not still be valid in light of events happening, so the project may need to be refocused. This is particularly true if your risk response strategies were not as effective as you'd like.

Question

Iris is an IT project manager in a manufacturing company. She has to use a new CAD – computer aided design – system for her next project, which involves precise engineering. The project involves a system upgrade.

Match risk response strategies Iris could take in this situation to the examples that illustrate them.

Options:
- A. Transference
- B. Avoidance
- C. Mitigation
- D. Acceptance

Targets:
1. Iris can hire a CAD systems specialist contractor to perform the upgrade
2. Iris could use a design system her team is already familiar with
3. Iris could hire someone who's experienced in CAD engineering to train her team and help with the project
4. Iris can acknowledge the fact that any upgrades may have small impacts on the project's internal deliverables

Answer

By hiring a third party contractor, Iris is transferring risk by transferring the responsibility for managing the upgrade process.

Using a proven design system, provided that it meets the customer's requirements, is a way for Iris to avoid the risks inherent with having to use an unfamiliar system.

If Iris has to use the new CAD system, adding an experienced resource and training her own personnel are ways to mitigate the risk.

With small impacts, Iris might choose to accept the risk or develop a contingency plan that describes how to reduce the impact if it happens.

4. Summary

In risk response planning, you review your prioritized list of potential project risks to determine what, if any, action should be taken. The four strategies in developing risk responses are transference, avoidance, mitigation, and acceptance. Each strategy can be used to reduce or eliminate a potential threat's impact on your project or its chance of occurrence.

Job Aid

Risk Response Strategies

Purpose: *Use this job aid as a reference to help you develop risk response strategies for IT projects.*

A table summarizing the strategies in developing risk responses	
Strategy	**Actions & Examples**
Transference	· Move the liability for the risk to a third party via insurance or contracts. · Use when you can't provide enough protection using other risk management options. · For example, use transference when your company lacks the required expertise or is located in an area prone to natural disasters.
Avoidance	· Change the project plan to eliminate the activity that created the risk. · Use with risks that are high impact and high or medium probability. · An example of avoidance is when you use tried and tested technology rather than new or untested technology.
Mitigation	· Find ways to reduce the risk's probability, impact, or both. · Use when you can't avoid a risk entirely, but wish to reduce its impact or likelihood. · Adding resources, using better-trained or more experienced person-

	nel, and using best practices are mitigation responses.
Acceptance	• Accept the consequences of the risk. • Use when you have a low impact and low probability risk, or when you can't transfer, avoid, or mitigate the risk. • When the risk is expected, and the level of impact to the project is within the tolerance level of the project team or organization, acceptance is an option. • If you can't reduce the risk to an acceptable level, if mitigation has resulted in residual risk that's still too great, or if the problem is outside the control of the project team, develop a contingency plan.

IT PROJECT MANAGEMENT ESSENTIALS: TESTING DELIVERABLES AND CLOSING IT PROJECTS

You've completed your project, and you're eager to move on to your next assignment. Your work is done, right? Actually, you may still have important work to do in order to properly close your project.

Closing your project properly is more than just something you should do – it's something you must do. The work you perform during this stage ensures that system functions are performed accurately, the system works with all interfacing systems, and that it meets requirements.

Before you close the project, you must first test the project deliverables. Testing is vital to ensure project requirements are met.

As the project manager, you can't move on to a new project until the testing processes have been carried out.

Once you've tested the project deliverables and confirmed that they meet the requirements, you can formally close the project. This phase has its own set of tasks, and is just as important as earlier phases. Completing these tasks helps increase the chances that the project will be a success.

But you're still not finished. Once testing has been completed and the project has been formally closed, it's time to set up maintenance and support for the client.

It's not enough to supply your customer with a new product; you must ensure that the solution continues to work properly after the project has been closed.

Setting up adequate maintenance and support means the difference between leaving the project behind and having to return to it later to troubleshoot and solve problems.

In this course, you'll learn about the steps involved in testing project deliverables, so you'll be able to ensure you're meeting project requirements.

Then, you'll find out what tasks help you properly close an IT project, including documenting lessons learned.

And finally, you'll learn the tasks involved in setting up maintenance and support to ensure continued support for the deliverable upon closure of the project.

Testing Deliverables and Closing IT Projects

1. Testing IT Project Deliverables
2. Closing an IT Project
3. Setting Up Maintenance and Support for IT Projects

TESTING IT PROJECT DELIVERABLES

1. Steps in testing deliverables

Testing is typically performed at the completion of a project and should also take place throughout the project's execution. This ensures that each stage is adequately tested before moving onto the next stage.

There are many types of tests you can use, each of which has its own specific function. Common tests include unit, usability, beta, regression, performance, benchmark and security.

Unit

Unit testing is completed throughout the entire project execution phase on software, hardware, processes, and procedures. Results of unit testing give you the first indication of how the project is progressing. An example of unit testing is when you want to validate that individual units of source code are working properly.

Usability

Usability testing is conducted in a controlled environment and is used to make sure your project's deliverable can be used in the real world. You might bring a small group of users into a testing environment to determine how users will interact with the deliverable in real life.

Beta

Beta testing involves issuing a limited release of the project's deliverables to a select group of users, which often includes expert testers who use the product as end users would.

Regression

Regression testing is performed after rework is completed to address errors and defects in the deliverable. It also ensures that fixes made to address the defects haven't introduced new issues.

Performance

Performance testing is used to determine how a component works when in actual use. There are four types of performance tests: stress, load, stability, and reliability. For instance, you could use performance testing to find out the expected load in terms of concurrent users or HTTP connections for a Web application.

Benchmark

Benchmark testing is used to test software or hardware against a specific performance standard, and can be performed during unit and integration testing, which is performed during reliability testing. Benchmark testing could involve testing against a known application that people are familiar with.

Security

Security testing should be performed on every IT project. It involves ensuring the project deliverables meet security requirements, as well as checking to make sure that the system can handle an attack, should one occur. Password cracking is an example of a security attack you might need to prevent.

When you're testing a project deliverable, you can follow five key steps. First, you identify the inputs that help ensure your testing is relevant for the system or product developed. Next, you identify appropriate testing tools. The third step is to design and implement the testing approach. Then, you obtain the desired outputs. Finally, you meet the milestones to move forward to the next phase or task.

It's important to note that some of these steps occur during different phases of the IT project. For instance, in the quality plan you'll identify the inputs, tools, and the approach to testing. You create the strategy at this point.

When it comes time to perform the testing, typically during the execution phase, you'll examine that plan and identify what you need to do.

In other words, even though the steps all relate to testing, they won't occur all at one time, but rather during different phases of the project.

The first step in the testing process involves **identifying five key inputs**: the corporate IT standards, the conversion plan, the data conversion process, the design document, and the requirements specifications. These inputs will help you determine the tools and approach you need to use for testing.

Corporate IT standards

The corporate IT standards are used to determine the set of testing tools to be used for the different testing stages.

Mark is the Project Manager for a project that is developing cruise control software for vehicles. He asks the team members to track test results in a database and use corporate certified hardware and software to test the code in the application.

Conversion plan

The conversion plan specifies the order in which parts of the application will be implemented, as well as the functionality that corresponds with each release.

Mark and his team decide that voice recognition, or VR, software will be integrated with the cruise control software only after it recognizes each command 100% of the time.

Data conversion process

The data conversion process documents the design of the application required to create the databases for the system.

Mark's team determines that a network-based data system will be created containing commands that the voice recognition software will be required to recognize.

Design document

The application flow and workflow sections of the design document are used during the testing phase to ensure that the product works as intended.

For example, the voice recognition software being created for a project will recognize commands given by the driver. Upon integration with the cruise control software, the VR software will translate the driver's spoken commands into machine-readable instructions that will engage the system.

Requirements specifications

The requirements specifications are used to ensure that the product meets all its functional and quality requirements.

For example, a process model may be used to show the process of software recognizing voice commands. An event model may also be created for the event that triggers the process, which is the driver speaking the command.

Question

Inputs are an important starting point for testing. Match each input to the appropriate example.

Options:

A.   Corporate IT standards
B.   Conversion plan
C.   Data conversion process
D.   Design document
E.   Requirements specifications

Targets:

1. Web-based tools will be used to test each component
2. Units will only be integrated after separate, successful tests
3. A web-based system will be created to store the information
4. Upon integration of the units, the software will calculate totals
5. Totals are accurately added after a user enters numbers

Answer

This is an example of corporate IT standards, which are used to determine the set of testing tools that will be used for various stages of testing.

This is an example of the conversion plan, which details the sequence in which parts of the application will be implemented, as well as the functionality corresponding to each release.

This is an example of the data conversion process, which documents the application design necessary for creating the system databases.

This is an example of information found in the design document. The application flow and workflow sections of the design document are used during the testing phase to ensure that the product works as intended.

This is an example of requirements specifications, which are used to ensure that the product meets all its functional and quality requirements.

The next step in the testing process is to **identify the tools** that can be used to test the system and track results. Standard tools – such as word processing software, and presentation and spreadsheet applications – can be used. You can also use other specialized tools, including specific testing software – such as those that only work with specific languages – bug-tracking databases, and source code control systems.

Testing tools are very specific to the types of environments, programs, and testing they are used for.

For example, web-based environments need web-based testing tools, such as HTTP requests to test a web application or a simple web browser.

Bug-tracking databases identify, categorize, log, and track the resolution of bugs or defects. Bugs and defects are problems in the system that would cause it to fail to meet a customer's or user's reasonable expectations of quality.

A bug–tracking system might be a database with a description of the problem, a rating, and a potential solution. You might also include the date and signature of the person reporting the bug.

Bug-tracking systems can be sophisticated systems that allow clients to connect to the corporate network, intranet, or Internet, and communicate with databases on a server or set of servers. Or they may be simple systems that run on a single, stand-alone PC or workstation.

Source code control systems are useful when different people are working on units of code at the same time. This helps you to avoid overwriting or undoing changes made by others.

For instance, you could implement versions of the product and assign version control to one person at a time.

Mark and his team set up a database to keep track of all the bugs and other issues that come up during the testing phase. They'll use it through the entire phase so the programmers will know which issues have been resolved and which still need attention.

Question

Now, check your understanding of the tools used during testing by matching each tool to its appropriate use.

Options:
   A.   Testing tools
   B.   Bug-tracking databases
   C.   Source code control systems

Targets:
   1. These verify that the system is functioning properly
   2. These manage errors found in a program
   3. These help manage different sections of code text for consistency

Answer

Testing tools are used to test the system and verify that it's functioning as it should.

Bug-tracking databases are tools that manage program errors. They identify, categorize, log, and track the resolution of bugs.

Source code control systems are tools that help maintain consistency when different people are working on units of code at the same time.

During the third step of the testing process, you **design and implement the testing approach**. This involves performing four key activities. First, you create the test plan. Next, you create the test model. Then you perform integration and user acceptance testing. Finally, you check the detailed results.

Create the test plan

Creating a test plan includes the specific testing to be performed, the test conditions, the test schedule, the expected results, and the personnel involved.

Creating the test plan also entails designing the testing approach. The purpose of this activity is to prepare for testing to take place, and to determine the level and types of testing.

Create the test model

Good test models or systems uncover the bugs that can hurt the deliverable in the market or reduce its acceptance by in-house users.

A test model defines testing processes, which include both written and unwritten procedures, checklists, and other agreements about the way the test team does its testing. The model also defines the tools, documents, scripts, data, cases, and tracking mechanisms that the test team uses to do its testing.

The test model includes the hardware, software, infrastructure, supplies, and facilities the test team uses to procure, install, and configure the system in order to test it.

Perform integration and user acceptance testing

The integration test verifies the accuracy of the communication among all programs in the new system. The user acceptance test simulates the actual working conditions of the new system, including the user manuals and procedures.

It's critical that the team ensures that the new system will work in the production environment. This means the team will require an operations guide showing how the new system is expected to work, as well as a troubleshooting guide that explains how to identify and fix problems with the system.

Check the detailed results

Checking the detailed results involves the project manager and team members finding out whether the system or product functions properly.

Sometimes it's unclear exactly what has gone wrong when an anomaly first comes to light. Further research is usually needed.

Mark, the project manager you met earlier in the topic, and his team must now design and implement the testing approach for their voice recognition software project:

1.   First, the programmers determine that they'll test each of the programming work units separately. The testing, which should take between four and eight hours, will result in units that function correctly 100% of the time.

2.   The team then obtains a simulated driving program that will be integrated with their application to test all functions. This will represent the production environment.

3.   Next, Mark's team tests each newly created combined unit until every unit has been integrated successfully. They also use the simulated driving program to test the user requirements.

4.   Finally, Mark and his team hold daily meetings to review the results of the unit test, the integrated test, and the system to ensure everything is functioning properly.

Mark and his team devised a test plan, created a test model, performed integration and user acceptance testing, and checked for detailed results.

By conducting these key testing activities, Mark and his team have increased the chances that they'll meet all the project's requirements.

Question

A project manager needs to design and implement the testing approach. To do this, she begins by testing each of the working units for a project separately, and then again as each unit is combined with another, until full integration is achieved. Quality specialists test the system as a whole to ensure that user requirements are functioning properly. A prototype of the system is developed for testing purposes. The project manager and project team meet to examine the outcomes and to ensure the entire system is working properly.

Have all the key activities of designing and implementing the testing approach been conducted?
Options:
1. No, the test plan and model have not been fully developed
2. Yes, all of the key activities have been conducted
3. No, the user acceptance testing has not been conducted

Answer

Option 1: *This is the correct option. Before she can implement the tests, the project manager needs to create a test plan and model based on the inputs and tools available for testing that particular project.*

Option 2: *This option is incorrect. The team didn't design a testing approach by creating a test plan and model.*

Option 3: *This option is incorrect. The team did in fact conduct user acceptance testing, but neglected to fully develop the test plan and model.*

The fourth step in the testing process is to **obtain the desired outputs**. This involves obtaining the test results, which are used as evidence that all the planned cycles have run successfully and that all outstanding issues have been resolved.

On Mark's project, the test results show that the voice recognition software does indeed recognize the commands spoken by the driver.

The results also show that the voice recognition software is able to translate the command into machine-readable instructions that the cruise control software can understand.

The final step in the testing phase involves **meeting the milestones** to move forward to the next phase or task. During this step, you must obtain a conversion readiness sign-off from the project's stakeholders. This involves obtaining the stakeholders' documented signatures.

After he shows them the results of the testing phase, Mark obtains conversion readiness sign-off from his department manager and from a representative of the automobile manufacturer.

Job Aid

Checklist for Testing IT Project Deliverables

Purpose: *Use this job aid as a checklist when testing your IT project deliverables.*

When you perform testing processes with your own products, use this checklist to ensure you've covered each of the steps and their associated activities.

STEP 1: IDENTIFY THE INPUTS

There are five key activities you'll perform during this step:

- use the corporate IT standards to determine the set of testing tools to be used for the different testing stages
- use the conversion plan to specify the order in which parts of the application will be implemented, as well as the functionality that corresponds with each release
- use the data conversion process to document the design of the application required to create the databases for the system
- use the application flow and workflow sections of the design document to ensure that the product works as intended
- use the requirements specifications to ensure that the product meets all its functional and quality requirements

STEP 2: IDENTIFY THE TOOLS

Tools that you may use include:

- testing tools are very specific to the types of environments, programs, and testing they are used for
- bug-tracking databases identify, categorize, log, and track the resolution of bugs
- source control systems are useful when different people are working on units of the code at the same time

STEP 3: DESIGN AND IMPLEMENT THE TESTING APPROACH

There are four key activities you'll perform during this step:
- create the test plan
- create the test model or system
- perform integration and user acceptance testing
- check the detailed results

STEP 4: OBTAIN THE DESIRED RESULTS

This step involves obtaining the test results, which are used as evidence that all the planned cycles have run successfully and that all outstanding issues have been resolved. If something is not functioning properly, further research will be needed to resolve the issue.

STEP 5: MEET THE MILESTONES TO MOVE FORWARD

During this step, you must obtain a conversion readiness sign-off form from the project's stakeholders.

Case Study: Question 1 of 2

Scenario

For your convenience, the case study is repeated with each question.

Vinny is the project manager on a project to upgrade his company's order-entry system software. Currently, he and his team are testing project deliverables.

Answer the questions in order.

Question

Match the first two steps involved in testing project deliverables with the corresponding activities that Vinny performs. Each step may match to more than one activity.

Options:

    A.   Identify the inputs

    B.   Identify the tools

Targets:

    1. Vinny uses corporate IT standards to determine the set of testing tools to be used for each testing stage

    2. Vinny outlines the requirements specifications to ensure that the new system meets all its functional and quality requirements

    3. Vinny and his team select bug-tracking databases to

identify, categorize, log, and track the resolution of bugs
4. Vinny chooses the set of tools used to test the system's functionality

Answer

Corporate standards are used during the first step – identify the inputs – to determine the set of testing tools to be used for the different testing stages.

Requirements specifications are used during the first step, which involves identifying the inputs, to ensure that the deliverable meets all its functional and quality requirements.

Bug-tracking databases are used during the second step, identify the tools, to identify, categorize, log, and track the resolution of bugs.

Testing tools are used during the second step – identify the tools – to test the system. They're very specific to the types of environments, programs, and testing being performed.

Case Study: Question 2 of 2

Scenario

For your convenience, the case study is repeated with each question.
Vinny is the project manager on a project to upgrade his company's order-entry system software. Currently, he and his team are testing project deliverables.

Answer the questions in order.

Question

Match the final three steps involved in testing project deliverables with the corresponding activities that Vinny performs. Each step may match to more than one activity.

Options:

A.   Design and implement the testing approach
B.   Obtain the desired outputs
C.   Meet the milestones

Targets:

1. Vinny and his team create the test model for the new order-entry system software
2. Vinny and his team find that the results of the tests

point to an anomaly that they need to resolve
3. Vinny obtains a conversion readiness sign-off from the department manager who will be using the new software
4. Vinny and his team perform an integration test to verify the accuracy of the communication among all programs in the new system

Answer

The test model is created during the third step – designing and implementing the testing approach.

The test results are obtained during the fourth step – obtaining the desired outputs. The test results are used as evidence that all the planned cycles have run successfully and that all outstanding issues have been resolved.

You obtain a conversion readiness sign-off from the project's stakeholders during the last step, meet the milestones to move forward to the next phase or task.

Integration and user acceptance testing are performed during the third step - to design and implement the testing approach. The integration test verifies the accuracy of the communication among all programs in the new system. The user acceptance test simulates the actual working conditions of the new system, including the user manuals and procedures.

2. Final Testing

Mark is a project manager who has just finished up his most recent project. He's feeling pleased with himself because all the design and development tasks for the project have been completed on time and under budget. Mark is ready to walk away from the project and move on to something new. However, he's neglected to perform a very important step prior to moving on to the next project – testing of the completed project deliverables.

Once all of the design and development tasks have been completed, the project manager and the project team must inspect their own work. A final testing phase is vital because it ensures that all requirements are met. Work conducted at this stage includes verifying that the functions are performed accurately, that the system works with all interfacing systems, and that the new system meets quality and standards requirements.

The purpose of testing prior to finalizing project close-out is to inspect the quality of the deliverables in the final product.

Throughout the design and development of an IT system or product, the project manager monitors quality.

When the system or product is finally developed or constructed, the project manager needs to test that it meets all the requirements to complete the project and that it integrates with the relevant systems.

Testing increases the chances that the project will be successful and the client will be satisfied with the final product.

Once the final quality test is completed, the project manager can move toward closing the project and setting up maintenance.

3. Summary

In an IT project, the testing process is vital because it ensures that all requirements are met, and increases the chances that the project will be successful. As project manager, your main task during testing is to inspect the quality of the project.

When you're testing a project deliverable, you must perform five key steps. First, you identify the inputs. Next, you identify the tools. The third step is to design and implement the testing approach. Then, you obtain the desired outputs. Finally, you meet the milestones to complete the process.

CLOSING AN IT PROJECT

1. Closing a project properly

How do you know when an IT project is really closed? There are several questions you can ask that will give you the answer. Has it been decided that the project goals have been met? Can no additional value be added to the project? Has the project been handed off to operations? And have all resources been released and reassigned? If the answer to these questions is "yes," then you can be sure the project is closed.

It's vital that you close each project properly. For one thing, it's beneficial for future projects when you properly archive and maintain documentation.

Closing a project properly also helps build a strong client relationship, as client satisfaction is more likely to be achieved when you ensure you have met all the client's requirements.

When you're closing a project, you should ensure that you complete all administrative closure. You need to gather all the documentation from the project, and ensure all contracts have been completed successfully so they can be closed and payments can be made.

Finally, make sure all the project information is available to everyone who can use it to learn from what you've done on the project.

The closing process helps you identify what worked and what didn't.

It's a good idea to step back and look at the actual data versus the planned data to determine what worked, what didn't work very well, what went terribly wrong, what crept up on you, and what worked surprisingly well.

Studying your project in retrospect will help you and your team learn a lot about many aspects of the project, the organization, and the team.

A project summary report, which is often a requirement, should be used in a positive, productive way.

You don't want to focus on the negative aspects or blame people. Instead, look at what worked, what didn't, and what can be improved for next time.

It's important to try to foster a culture where people feel comfortable admitting their shortcomings, errors, or omissions so that a better system can be created to avoid those problems in the future.

Question

What is the value of carrying out closing activities for an IT project?

Options:
1. You'll learn how to do things better on your next project
2. You'll be able to find out who is to blame for any errors
3. You'll be able to avoid performing administrative tasks related to closing
4. You'll be able to guarantee future project success

Answer

Option 1: *This is the correct option. Closing an IT project properly can teach you how to do things better on the next project because the closing process helps you identify what went right and what went wrong.*

Option 2: *This option is incorrect. Closing activities should be positively focused. Find out what went right, what went wrong, and focus on improving in the future.*

Option 3: *This option is incorrect. Administrative closure is an important part of closing a project. You need to gather all the documentation from the project, and ensure all contracts have been completed successfully so they can be closed and final payments can be* *made.*

Option 4: *This option is incorrect. Although past information can help you perform better in the future, there's never a guarantee that a project will be successful.*

2. Closing phase activities

When you're closing a project, there are five key steps you should follow. First, you must get formal acceptance. Then, you need to archive documentation and close contracts. Next, you have to write a post-implementation report. Finally, you should document lessons learned.

The first step in the closing process involves **getting formal acceptance** from the project stakeholders. After you've tested the deliverable in the production environment, you bring the stakeholders together for one final review of the project and its product.

At this point, you should go over any changes made to requirements or scope. This will ensure that everyone is in agreement about their expectations for the project.

If any changes or additions are requested at this point, shift the focus back to what was originally agreed upon and requested in the project plan. The project would go on indefinitely if changes or additions were accepted.

Question

Which activities are performed during the getting formal acceptance step of the closing process?

Options:

1. Have the stakeholders perform one final review of the project
2. Go over any changes made to requirements or scope
3. Focus on what was originally agreed upon and requested in the project plan
4. Archive documentation
5. Document lessons learned

Answer

Option 1: *This option is correct. After you've tested the deliverable in* *the production environment, you bring the stakeholders together for one final review of the project.*

Option 2: *This option is correct. At this point, you should go over any changes made to requirements or scope. This will ensure that everyone is in agreement about their expectations for the project.*

Option 3: *This option is correct. If any changes or additions are requested at this point, shift the focus back to what was originally agreed upon and requested in the project plan.*

Option 4: *This option is incorrect. Archiving documentation is not an activity performed while getting formal acceptance.*

Option 5: *This option is incorrect. Documenting lessons learned is the final step in the closing phase, not something you do while getting final acceptance.*

During the next step in the closing phase, you need to **archive documentation**. There's a large amount of information you need to gather during the project, including project-related plans, reports, contract files, and legal documentation. If you have kept these documents up to date as the project progressed, this information should be readily available.

One way to archive your documentation is to set up a database that can be searched by anyone who needs to access this information.

This database can provide you with all sorts of information about the project – for instance, which contractors always deliver on time and to specifications.

Question

Which activities are performed when you archive documentation as part of closing a project?

Options:

1. Gather information such as project-related plans, reports, and contract files
2. Set up a searchable database
3. Go over any changes made to requirements or scope
4. Write a post-implementation report

Answer

Option 1: *This option is correct. There's a large amount of information you need to gather during the project, including project-related plans, reports, contract files, and legal documentation.*

Option 2: *This option is correct. One way to archive your documentation is to set up a database that can be searched by anyone who needs to access this information.*

Option 3: *This option is incorrect. This is an activity you perform during the previous step, which involves getting formal acceptance.*

Option 4: *This option is incorrect. It is not necessary to archive documentation before writing the report.*

Along with getting formal acceptance and archiving documentation, you also need to **close the contracts**. A contract is a legal agreement between you and a business or individual who has supplied you with goods or services.

Before a contract can be closed, all parties must be in agreement. Your company may have a contracting or procurement department, which handles the administrative details involved with closing the contracts.

However, as the project manager, you still have to verify that the contractor has completed all work to your satisfaction.

This means you need to review whether deliverables were completed on time to the quality required. You should also confirm that the work was completed within the agreed upon budget.

If your company does not have a procurement department, you are responsible for ensuring that all administrative items are addressed.

These include ensuring that the contractor has received all payments due, and that there are no outstanding change orders to the contract.

If you have only labor contracts – for example, you hired programmers who were paid an hourly wage – then there is typically not too much paperwork. However, if you contracted a large chunk of the project or purchased components, you'll want to make certain that the work is as expected.

Question

Which activities are performed during the closing contracts step?

Options:

1. Ensure that all parties involved in the contract are in agreement
2. Verify that the work was completed to the specifications
3. Ensure that deliverables were completed on time, within budget, and to the expected quality
4. Have the stakeholders perform one final review of the project
5. Gather information such as project-related plans, reports, and contract files

Answer

Option 1: This option is correct. Before a contract can be closed, all parties must be in agreement.

Option 2: This option is correct. As the project manager, you must verify that the contractor has completed all work to your satisfaction.

Option 3: This option is correct. You must ensure that deliverables were completed on time and with acceptable quality. You should also confirm that the work was completed within the agreed upon budget.

Option 4: This option is incorrect. This is an activity performed when you are getting formal acceptance.

Option 5: This option is incorrect. You gather information such as project-related plans, reports, and contract files when you are archiving documentation.

Another closing activity is **writing a post-implementation report**, or summary report. This report gives you a chance to draw attention to what went well in your project, or to identify areas that were problematic so you can improve next time. It can be as short as a few paragraphs for a small project, or many pages long in the case of a larger project.

Before you write your report, you should have a project review meeting to recap the project.

You could also send out surveys asking team members for their feedback about the project before you write the report.

So what exactly should your summary report contain? There are many areas you could cover, but some of the most common include project effectiveness, project management processes, risk management, communication management, project implementation, performance of the project team, and key metrics.

Project effectiveness

In the project effectiveness section, you'll summarize how effectively your project met the customer's needs. You should highlight any specific product performance metrics here, as well as outliers – the stakeholder groups who are either very satisfied or very dissatisfied with the product.

Project management processes

The project management processes section should outline the effectiveness of your project management processes throughout the project. For instance, how were approved changes to project scope managed? How did the baseline schedule and budget compare to the final versions?

Risk management

In the risk management section, you'll summarize how effectively you managed risk during the project. You should include any significant risks that actually occurred, and how well your mitigation plan worked. You should also identify any outliers with regard to your risk management process.

Communication management

The communication management section should describe the effectiveness of the communications plan that was developed for the project. Were there any communications activities that were especially effective? Were there any specific issues with regard to communications that had to be addressed?

Project implementation

In the project implementation section, you'll discuss how effectively the project was implemented, as well as the success of the transition period. You should describe any significant milestones that occurred during this phase, and the effectiveness of the activities you had planned for those milestones.

Performance of the project team

The performance of the project team should be outlined in this section. Was the project team effective? What were the team's responsibilities, and how well were they accomplished?

Key metrics

The key metrics section describes specific metrics depending on what you used during your project execution. Some examples include cost, schedule, scope, and quality.

Question

Which activities do you carry out when writing a post-implementation, or summary, report?

Options:

1. Hold a project review meeting to recap the project
2. Include key areas such as project effectiveness and risk management
3. Gather information such as project-related plans, reports, and contract files
4. Document lessons learned

Answer

Option 1: *This option is correct. Before you write your report, you should have a project review meeting to recap the project. You could also send out surveys asking team members for their feedback about the project before you write the report.*

Option 2: *This option is correct. There are many areas your report could cover, but some of the most common include project effectiveness, project management processes, risk management, communication management, project implementation, performance of the project team, and key metrics.*

Option 3: *This option is incorrect. This is an activity you perform when archiving documentation.*

Option 4: *This option is incorrect. Documenting lessons learned is the final step when you're closing an IT project. You'll learn about this step next.*

You've gone through all the steps in the closing phase except the final one – **documenting lessons learned**. Drawing on your summary report and issues you may have logged during the course of the project, you reflect on why some things went well and others didn't. Then you document the "lessons," including what you need to do in the future to improve. Ideally, you'll have done this throughout each phase of the project, but at the very least, you should perform this step once the project is over.

It's useful at this point to hold an informal, wrap-up meeting to review the lessons learned, the context of the lessons learned, the improvements that can be made, and the positive things that worked and should be done again in the future. If the meeting is informal, people are more likely to be relaxed and feel like they can tell you their thoughts without fear of reprimand.

While the meeting should be informal, it's still important to prepare a loose agenda. In order to pinpoint the lessons learned, you might want to ask a few questions:

- What went well on the project, and why?
- What could we have done better?
- Was there anything that went differently than planned?
- Are there any ways in which the project team could have worked better together?
- Were there any serious issues that came up during the project?
- What are the most valuable lessons learned on this project?

Job Aid

Closing an IT Project

Purpose: *Use this job aid as a checklist when closing your IT project.*
When you're closing an IT project, there are five key steps you should follow. During each of these steps, you should perform certain activities and ask key questions to ensure you're closing your project properly.

STEP 1: GET FORMAL ACCEPTANCE

- After you've tested the deliverable in the production environment, you bring the stakeholders together for one final review of the project and product.
- Go over any changes made to requirements or scope to ensure that everyone is in agreement about their expectations for the project.
- If any changes or additions are requested at this point, shift the focus back to what was originally agreed upon and requested in the project plan.

STEP 2: ARCHIVE DOCUMENTATION

- Set up a database that can be searched by anyone who needs to access project-related information, such as project-related plans, reports, contract files, and legal documentation.

STEP 3: CLOSE THE CONTRACTS

- Before a contract can be closed, all parties must be in agreement.
- Verify that the contractor has completed all work to your satisfaction.
- Ensure that deliverables were completed on time and with acceptable quality.
- Confirm that the work was completed within the agreed upon budget.

STEP 4: WRITE A POST-IMPLEMENTATION REPORT

- Before you write your report, have a project review meeting to recap the project and send out surveys asking team members for their feedback about the project.
- Your report should include these key areas:

  - project effectiveness
    - project management processes
    - risk management
    - communication
    - project implementation
    - performance of the project team
    - key metrics

STEP 5: DOCUMENT LESSONS LEARNED

- Review the post-implementation report and identify problems, as well as things that worked. Document lessons learned from these problems and the positives.
- Hold an informal meeting to get the views of the team and create a relaxed environment so people are more likely to be relaxed and feel like they can tell you their thoughts without fear of reprimand.
- During the meeting, ask key questions about the project:

  - What went well on the project, and why?
  - What could we have done better?
  - Was there anything that went differently than planned?
  - Are there any ways in which the project team could have worked better together?
  - Were there any serious issues that came up during the project?
  - What are the most valuable lessons learned on this project?

Examples of some of the issues that could come up during the session include problems resulting from incomplete or unclear project definitions.

The lesson learned from this problem might include spending more time with stakeholders in advance of project planning.

You might also experience problems stemming from inaccurate

or unrealistic scheduling or budgeting. A lesson learned here might be to include the finance department and subject matter experts in developing a more refined project budget.

Case Study: Question 1 of 2

Scenario

For your convenience, the case study is repeated with each question.

Tom is the project manager on a project to develop organizational documentation templates. The project is drawing to a close, and Tom must perform the closing phase activities.

Answer the questions in order.

Question

Which examples illustrate activities Tom performs to get formal acceptance, archive documentation, and close contracts?

Options:

1. Tom brings all of the department managers together for one final review of the templates
2. Tom creates a database that contains all the information used to create the templates
3. Tom settles all invoices from the contractors hired to help with the project
4. Tom makes changes as requested by key stakeholders
5. Tom closes all the contracts even though one contractor disputes a specific charge on her invoice

Answer

Option 1: This option is correct. The first step in the closing process involves getting formal acceptance from the project stakeholders. After you've tested the deliverables in the production environment, you bring the stakeholders together for one final review of the project and product.

Option 2: This option is correct. The second step involves archiving documentation. There's a large amount of information you need to gather during the project, including project-related plans, reports, contract files, and legal documentation. One way to manage this information is with a searchable database.

Option 3: This option is correct. The third step in the closing process is to close the contracts. A contract is a legal agreement between you and a business or individual who has supplied you with goods or services.

Option 4: This option is incorrect. If any changes or additions are requested by stakeholders at this point, you should shift the focus back to what was originally agreed upon and requested in the project plan.

Option 5: This option is incorrect. Before a contract can be closed, all parties must be in agreement.

Case Study: Question 2 of 2

Scenario

For your convenience, the case study is repeated with each question.
Tom is the project manager on a project to develop organizational documentation templates. The project is drawing to a close, and Tom must perform the closing phase activities.
Answer the questions in order.

Question

Which examples describe activities Tom should perform when writing a post-implementation or summary report and documenting lessons learned?

Options:

1. Tom writes a report specifying that the project was a success, but just missed coming in under budget
2. Tom books a meeting room at an offsite location such as at a hotel where lunch and snacks are provided
3. Tom checks the documents against the project management plan and has the stakeholders review and give their acceptance of the results
4. Tom gathers information such as project-related plans, reports, and contract files

Answer

Option 1: This option is correct. The fourth step in the closing process is to write a post-implementation report, which gives you a chance summarize how the project went.

Option 2: This option is correct. The final step in the closing process is to document lessons learned. It's useful at this point to hold an

informal meeting so team members are more likely to be relaxed and feel like they can tell you their thoughts without fear of reprimand.
Option 3: *This option is incorrect. This activity is part of getting formal acceptance of project deliverables.*
Option 4: *This option is incorrect. This is an activity Tom would have performed when he was archiving documentation.*

3. Summary

It's vital that you close each project properly. It's beneficial for future projects when you properly archive and maintain documentation, and it can help build a strong client relationship. By properly closing a project, you'll learn how to do things better on the next project because the closing process helps you identify what went right and what went wrong.

When you're closing a project, there are five key activities to perform. You must get formal acceptance, archive documentation, and clo

Follow-on Activity
Project Close-out Report
Purpose: *Use this follow-on activity to design your own project close-out report.*
Using information specific to projects at your own company, design a project close-out report. You can either design this based on an upcoming project, or for a project you've worked on in the past.
You may design this report to your own specifications, but you may wish to include information about what went well and what could be improved in these areas:

- project scope
- project deliverables
- overall direction of the project
- project teams
- project logistics
- life cycle of the project
- risk management

- overall assessment
- areas specific to your project

SETTING UP MAINTENANCE AND SUPPORT FOR IT PROJECTS

1. Maintenance and support

So you've completed all the acceptance testing trials for your IT project and carried out key closing activities. What happens next? Now it's time for the information systems support group to take responsibility for the maintenance and support of the system. This group can either be an internal part of your organization, or the task can be handed over to the company providing the support function for your organization.

Many project managers believe that their project is a success if it's completed on time, within budget, and to specifications. But it's also important to prevent the project from failing after completion.

That's why adequate support is vital after a project is closed – to ensure the project continues to be a success even after it's been formally signed off.

In the IT industry, project teams are still connected to their providing companies, even after they're finished.

Customers don't just pay for a product or service; they also pay for – and expect – continued support and maintenance, even after the product or service is delivered.

The type of support required can vary greatly, depending on the solution and the level of complexity of the system being provided. It's your responsibility as project manager to ensure that your client understands the full requirements and level of support that will be required to maintain the solution.

In order to determine what type of maintenance and support is appropriate for a particular solution, you can ask yourself a few questions:

- Does the product or system include full-time, affordable support?
- Has the client budgeted appropriately for any software licensing fees that will be due annually?
- Has the client ordered the necessary hardware spares and accessories for the system?
- Does the client have the necessary hardware and storage capacity for future expansion?
- Have helpdesk employees been trained to handle calls from system users?

2. Setting up maintenance and support

When you thought about what you need to do to set up maintenance and support for an IT project, you may have thought of some of these tasks – activating helpdesk support, developing a formal service level agreement, and estimating when the next change will occur.

One task in setting up maintenance and support is **activating helpdesk support**. Many systems require a helpdesk function, and you should include developing and delivering training to helpdesk staff as part of your project schedule.

You'll need to figure out when the helpdesk group will begin taking calls. This usually occurs once the new system is deployed to end users.

If end users will be receiving the new system on a staggered schedule, you must ensure all users have access to adequate helpdesk coverage.

When you're activating helpdesk support, don't forget to prominently display the helpdesk phone number on all relevant applications or on a specific web site, so it's easy for users to access. Help desk staff should have access to any phone numbers needed to contact staff, suppliers, and contractors who support the solution. You should also provide helpdesk staff with a list of possible problems that users could run into, so they're prepared to deal with any issues.

Peter is the project manager for a project that will provide and configure laptops for his client's sales team. Follow along as he speaks with Janine, the helpdesk supervisor.

> **Peter:** Hi Janine. I wanted to let you know that the sales team received their laptops this morning, so you can expect calls to start coming in later today.

> **Janine:** Thanks Peter. I feel like we're ready, but it's always hard to know what kind of problems will come up.

> **Peter:** I've prepared a document that covers some common problems you might run into. I've left a copy on each of your team members' desks – that should help you a bit.

> **Janine:** That should be really useful – thanks!

> **Peter:** I'm also going to send out an e-mail with a list of phone numbers you can call for help with specific technical issues if you can't solve them yourselves.

> **Janine:** That's great. I feel like we're prepared for anything!

By providing her with a list of potential problems, as well as contact numbers she can use in case of unforeseen issues, Peter gave Janine and her helpdesk team the tools they need to provide adequate support to the sales team as they set up their new laptops.

Question
Which examples illustrate activities performed when you activate helpdesk support?
Options:
1. Set up a day-long training session for the three employees who will be working at the helpdesk

2. Determine that the helpdesk will begin taking calls on the same day the product is delivered to the client
3. Affix a sticker displaying the helpdesk phone number to all copies of the new software
4. Provide the helpdesk with the project deliverable helpdesk support information so they can create helpdesk documentation
5. Give helpdesk staff instructions for looking up any phone numbers they might need in case of problems

Answer

Option 1: *This option is correct. Many systems require a helpdesk function, and you should include developing and delivering training to helpdesk staff as part of your project schedule.*

Option 2: *This option is correct. You'll need to figure out when the helpdesk group will begin taking calls; this usually occurs once the new system is deployed to end users. If multiple end users will be receiving the new system on a staggered schedule, you must ensure all users have adequate helpdesk coverage.*

Option 3: *This option is correct. When you're activating helpdesk support, don't forget to prominently display the helpdesk number on all relevant applications or on a specific web site, so it's easy for users to access.*

Option 4: *This option is incorrect. The helpdesk support team should not be responsible for writing the documentation.*

Option 5: *This option is incorrect. Actually, you should provide helpdesk staff members with any phone numbers they might need to contact staff, suppliers, and contractors who support the solution, should it fail.*

When setting up maintenance and support, you also need to **develop a formal service level agreement**. It might seem like a simple formality, but creating a formal agreement between the organization and suppliers is vital to maintaining continued support and service.

The service level agreement is a negotiated document that defines, in quantitative terms, the service being provided to the customer. It should fully define the services to be supplied and the service quality and timeliness or responsiveness associated with them in clear terms.

The agreement should contain metrics that can be measured on a regular basis. It should also specify who exactly will record these metrics.

Examples of metrics that are typically included in the service level agreement are service hours and availability, customer support levels, any restrictions that might exist, and functionality.

You can think of the service level agreement as a type of assurance or warranty. It specifies the level of service that will be delivered to the client. You should periodically review the service level agreement, and renegotiate whenever there's a change to requirements or you're not able to meet a requirement.

Peter, the project manager you met earlier in this topic, meets with the procurement manager at his client's company to discuss the level of service that will be provided for the new laptops.

The formal service level agreement specifies that Peter's company will provide warranty service on the units for one year. After that period, the client will be responsible for its own service requirements.

The agreement also specifies that Peter's company will provide helpdesk support for technical issues until all staff members have completely set up the required software on their laptops.

Question

What are the tasks involved in developing a service level agreement?

Options:

1. Define the specific level of service being provided to the customer
2. Specify who will record metrics such as functionality, customer support levels, and hours of availability
3. Include information about when you estimate the next change to the product or service will occur

4. Ensure that the service level agreement includes information about how to contact the helpdesk

Answer

Option 1: This option is correct. The service level agreement is a negotiated document that defines, in quantitative terms, the service being provided to the customer.

Option 2: This option is correct. The service level agreement should contain metrics that can be measured on a regular basis. It should also specify who exactly will record these metrics. Examples of metrics that are typically included in the service level agreement are service hours and availability, customer support levels, any restrictions that might exist, and functionality.

Option 3: This option is incorrect. Estimating when the next change will occur is not part of developing a service level agreement but is a key task in setting up maintenance and support.

Option 4: This option is incorrect. This is something you would have done when setting up helpdesk support, not developing the service level agreement.

When setting up maintenance and support, you also need to **estimate when the next change will occur**. It's inevitable that soon after you complete a project, you'll have to start thinking about upgrades and enhancements.

As project manager, it's your job to estimate when these enhancements and upgrades will be available.

Most technology has a limited life span, and you need to plan for the costs associated with upgrading. You should forward these costs to the operations manager or the executive team that will be taking ownership of the system when it goes live.

Since these costs will be sure to come up in the future, having a rough estimate of when they'll be necessary will help with budgeting and planning.

Peter knows there will be a new operating system available in a year and recommends to his client that they should plan to upgrade all staff laptops at that time. This will be a significant expense, and he sends a written estimate to the operations manager for budgeting and planning purposes.

Question
What tasks do you perform when setting up maintenance and support for completed IT projects?
Options:
1. Develop training for helpdesk staff as part of your project schedule
2. Plan for the costs associated with inevitable upgrades
3. Only include current technology needs in the budget
4. Create a document that defines the service being provided to the customer
5. Have an informal agreement in place with suppliers that loosely outlines the level of service that will exist

Answer
Option 1: *This option is correct. A key task in setting up maintenance and support is to activate helpdesk support. Many systems require a helpdesk function, and you should include developing and delivering training to helpdesk staff as part of your project schedule.*

Option 2: *This option is correct. Most technology has a limited life span before it becomes outdated, and you need to plan for the costs associated with upgrading by estimating when the next change will occur.*

Option 3: *This option is incorrect. Most technology has a limited life span before it becomes outdated, and you need to plan for the costs associated with upgrading.*

Option 4: *This option is correct. The service level agreement is a negotiated document that defines, in quantitative terms, the service being provided to the customer.*

Option 5: *This option is incorrect. When setting up maintenance and support, you need to develop a formal service level agreement that defines, in quantitative terms, the service being provided to the customer.*

3. Summary
Just because your project was completed on time, within budget,

and to specifications, doesn't mean it was a success. Many IT projects fail in the weeks following formal sign-off, which is why adequate support is vital after the project is closed.

Customers expect continued support and maintenance, even after the product or service is delivered. It's your responsibility as project manager to ensure that your client understands the full requirements and level of support that will be required to maintain the solution.

To set up maintenance and support for your IT project, you must perform three tasks – activate helpdesk support, develop a formal service level agreement, and estimate when the next change will occur.

Printed in Poland
by Amazon Fulfillment
Poland Sp. z o.o., Wrocław
28 February 2023

64ddeaa0-da12-40e5-b629-36655de0deccR01